# LIFE AND TRADITION ON
## THE COTSWOLDS

# LIFE & TRADITION
## on the
# COTSWOLDS

## by EDITH BRILL

with 243 photographs
19 drawings
and a map

LONDON: J. M. DENT & SONS LTD

First published 1973

© Edith Brill 1973

Made in Great Britain
by
W & J Mackay Limited, Chatham
for
J. M. DENT & SONS LTD
Aldine House · Albemarle Street · London

ISBN: 0 460 07861 5

# Contents

# Photographs

# Drawings

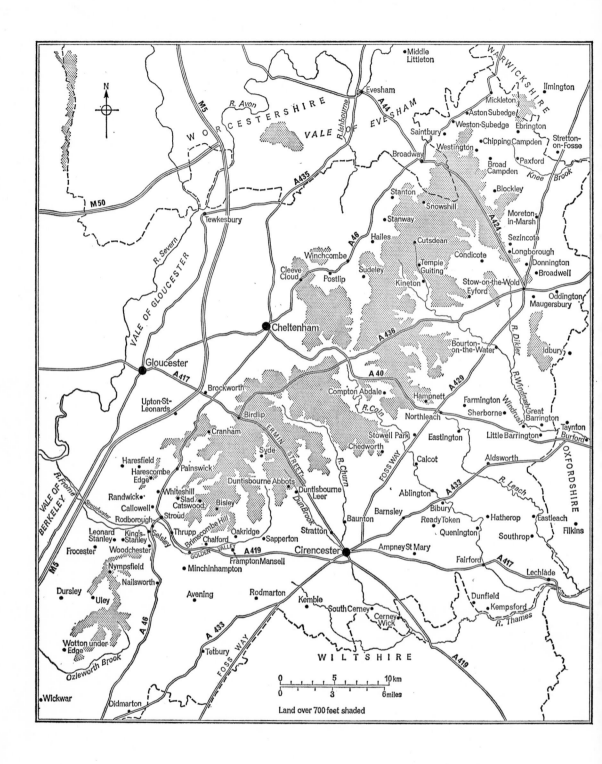

Land over 700 feet shaded

# Author's Acknowledgments

My greatest debt is to Peter and June Turner: Peter, who has taken the majority of the photographs and June for her many discoveries of records and relics of the past hidden away on the farms of her friends and acquaintances. I have also to thank them for their sustained enthusiasm and encouragement.

Mr George Swinford, master mason, not only gave me permission to use as illustrations any exhibits from his Museum at Filkins but in our talks brought to life the old craftsmen who made them by his intimate knowledge and concern. Mr Don Keyte, wheelwright and carpenter of Paxford, also helped me in this way, as did Mr James Strange, of Westington Quarries, Campden.

For permission to use photographs both old and new I am indebted to: Major and Mrs Anthony Biddulph, Rodmarton, Pls 8, 68, 70, 71, 72, 73, 74, 129, 131, 132, 134, 135; Mr G. S. Cullimore, Pls 189, 190; Mr C. Curtis, Pl. 153; Mr W. Gardner, Pls 225, 226; Miss C. Guerrier, Pls 29, 30, 98, 136, 234, 235, 236, 237, 238; Mrs M. E. Heaven, Pl. 19; Mr W. R. James, Pls 50, 137, 146, 147, 148, 149; *Evesham Journal*, Pl. 243; Mrs F. King, Pls 20, 38, 103, 105, 169; Mr P. King, Pls 175, 183, 184, 185; Mr R. T. B. Martin, Pls 100, 101, 102, 104, 106, 120, 121, 122; Mr G. B. Mayo, Pls 86, 87; *Sunday Mercury*, Pls 191, 192, 193, 194, 195; Mr J. Millard, Pls 88, 89, 90, 91; Mr Nurding, Pl. 58; Mrs Parnham, Pl. 63; Mr Gilbert Peachy, Pls 212, 213, 214, 215; Mr E. Pearce, Pls 66, 92; Mr J. Philips, Pl. 182; Mr A. Pullin, Pls 95, 96, 97, 168; Mr F. T. Pullin, Pls 93, 94; Mrs M. G. Richardson, Pls 43, 51, 123, 155; Mrs Bernard Righton, Pl. 107; Mr Fred Saunders, Pls 114, 115, 116, 118, 228; Miss Victoria Smith, Pls 54, 76, 77, 78, 80, 81, 83, 142, 156, 174; Mr H. Steel, Pls 143, 163; Stowell Park Workshops, Pls 182, 221, 223; Mr R. Soule, Pls 109, 117, 138, 139, 140, 154, 173, 227; Mrs P. Turner, Pl. 69; Mr W. H. Taylor, Pls 34, 35; Mrs W. H. Taylor, Pl. 61; Mr and Mrs A. Twinning, Pls 59, 60, 67, 141, 144, 145, 160, 186, 188, 216, 217, 218, 219; Mr R. H. Wilcox, Pls 40, 41, 42; Mrs M. Wooldridge, Pl. 47; also to the Curator of the Stroud Museum for finding us a barley hummeller (Pl. 159).

Besides these I have to thank Mr Ian Forster of Campden for his architectural drawings, and Mr Tom Chadwick for his drawings of exhibits from Filkins Museum and Town Farm, Ebrington, as well as permission to use his drawings of Ebrington church clock and the old waggon.

Lt-Col. R. B. Mills of Barrington Grove has kindly allowed me to use his private Ms on the History of the Strongs and Kempsters, master masons of the Burford area, and Mr Norman Jewson to quote from his book *By Chance I Did Rove*.

It is impossible to thank individually the many people who over the years have made the compiling of this book possible and pleasurable, mostly country folk who have told me about Cotswold life as they knew it in their young years or who searched their memories for tales told to them by their elders when they were young. I hope those who are still living will accept this small tribute to their friendship and patience.

E.B.

# I

# THE BUILDINGS

*'On the Cotswolds the stone is in the blood.' Freda Derrick*

1. *Edge Quarry.*

2. *A ploughed field near Paxford.*

3. *Swells Hill from Brimscombe Hill, with Stroud in the background.*

4. *Cranham Woods in winter.*

5. *A typical Cotswold house at Weston Sub-edge.*

6. *A modern house built in traditional style and materials, Minchin-hampton.*

7. *House of the 1970s in substitute materials but not entirely forsaking tradition, Minchin-hampton.*

8. *Rodmarton Manor. Cotswold revival, perfected in detail.*

9. *Jacobean house in Winchcombe.*

10. *High Street, Bisley.*

11. *Urban vernacular: Chipping Campden.*

12–15. *Cirencester. Left and right above, either side of Thomas Street. Left below, at the corner of Coxwell Street; right below, Coxwell Street.*

16–18. *Cirencester. Dollar Street; Park Street; Cecily Hill.*

19. *Seventeenth-century doorway at Street Farm, Nympsfield.*

20. *Porch at Little Britain Farm, Woodchester, with stone seats and a room above.*

21. *Lintel porch at Great Barrington.*

22. *Shell-headed porch, Cossack Square, Nailsworth.*

23. *Design for a semicircular terrace of four cottages and a schoolroom built for John Chamberlayne at Maugersbury in 1800.*

24. *Cottages at Little Barrington.*

25. *Churnside cottages, South Cerney.*

26. *Cottage at Sherborne incorporating monastic remains.*

27–28. *Eighteenth-century weavers' cottages, Atcombe Terrace, South Woodchester, with enlarged 'weaving' window.*

29-30. *Ebrington village street about 1900, with rickyards on either side showing the continuity of pre-eighteenth-century farming when farmhouses were situated within the main part of the village.*

31. *The formerly imposing entrance to Ansted's Farm, Catswood, Bisley.*

32. *A complex of stone-slated farm buildings near Winchcombe.*

33. *Farmhouse with timbering, Weston Subedge.*

34–35. *Wades Farm, Slad Valley, Stroud, contains an ancient stone staircase.*

36. *Knapp House Farm, The Vatch, Slad Valley, Stroud.*

37. *Barn and yard near Hatherop.*

38. *Farmyard, Little Britain Farm, Woodchester.*

39. *Large barn at Kemble.*

40–42. *Manor Farm, Baunton, near Cirencester. Entrance, yard, and interior of barn.*

# Introduction

COTSWOLD covers an area of hill country roughly forty miles long and twenty miles broad, lying north of Wotton under Edge, east of Gloucester and Cheltenham, bordered by Fairford and Burford in the south-east and Campden in the north. One cannot say to a few miles where Cotswold begins or ends, its devotees holding vigorous opinions on the subject, but the main part is contained in Gloucestershire with a considerable lapping over into Oxfordshire and fringing Worcestershire, Warwickshire, Wiltshire and Somerset. Outside Gloucestershire the region is more receptive to lowland influences and its unique character becomes diluted.

It is generally accepted that Cotswold was derived from *Cod*, a personal Saxon name, and *wald* meaning forest or woodland. Natural beechwoods, western outliers of chalk-down beechwoods, once covered a considerable area of South Cotswold, and the rest of the region would have been covered with light woodland and oolitic scrub before it was cleared by grazing animals and cultivation. Shakespeare's 'Cotsal' is still used locally; the eighteenth and nineteenth centuries elaborated it into Cotteswold and Cotteswolde according to individual fancy; the twentieth century has finalized it into Cotswold.

The height of the hills ranges from 300 feet to just over 1,000 feet at Cleeve Cloud above Cheltenham; the high wolds average 700 to 900 feet, with the plateau in the north passing into wolds of lesser altitude as they fall gradually into the basins of the Thames and the Bristol Avon. Their most dramatic feature is the great escarpment seen from beyond Severn as an unbroken rampart on the horizon: a closer view shows it as cut into numerous steep-sided fissures, some with streams in the bottom, others forming narrow dry valleys with precipitous slopes. Beechwoods, western outliers of chalk-down beechwoods, clothe the slopes from Birdlip to a little beyond Dursley and provide a darker emphasis to the naturally dark tones of wold landscape. For centuries the wolds were unenclosed sheepwalks; today the vast fields of wheat and barley which have replaced the sheepwalks still keep some of that ancient amplitude, the drystone walls enclosing them barely interrupting the flowing contours of the hills, it being a quality of the local stone to fade into the landscape rather than intrude upon it.

The edge of the escarpment forms a marked climatic divide. Normally the hills are two to three degrees colder than the vale, but winter is much colder, with January and February the coldest months, and cold winds and frost often continue well into May. Over Gloucestershire generally an eastern air movement prevails and climatically Cotswold is distinguished from the Vale of Severn by its greater rainfall, decrease in temperature, the bite and bleakness of its winds; autumns, however, are often prolonged and leaf-fall delayed. Late frosts mean that fruit growing is a chancy business, except on the lower slopes.

A local saying for an event slow to materialize is 'as long coming as Cotswold barley', though Cobbett in his *Rural Rides*, commenting on the winter wheat he saw in October 1835, said that 'in places it was high enough to hide a hare', and far in advance of crops he noticed on lowland farms, the result of good husbandry and because the seed had been sown at the right time. Cobbett, and most others at that period, saw little beauty in the Cotswold landscape; it was too austere for one nurtured in a more benign southern county and his real appreciation of natural beauty was not moved by its bare solitudes. Describing a newly ploughed field, he was seeing it with a farmer's eye when he remarked: 'The soil is what is called stone brash below, with reddish earth mixed with little bits of this brash on top, and for the greater part of the wold even this soil is very shallow'. Anyone who knows Cotswold cannot fail to recognize his description, and a lover of the region would also see the orange tones of newly-turned earth giving a warm glow to acre after acre stretching to the horizon in a beauty of line and living colour.

An old lady in her eighties once told me how she remembered as a girl watching the women of the village waiting in line to be taken on by the local farmers to pick stones off the fields, not the small flakes making up at least eighty per cent of the surface soil but larger pieces of rock which would get in the way of the plough or seed-drill. When there was no other work for the women there was always stone-picking because the fields could never be cleared. The stones 'growed' each year like weeds, she told me, as anyone could see after the first ploughing of the season.

The hills need their greater rainfall. The brash and the rock beneath are porous and the ground rarely becomes sour or water-logged. The flakes of stone littering the surface keep the topsoil from being dried out by the ever-persistent winds. In a dry summer great cracks in the wheat and barley fields have no effect upon crops whose roots are held far down in the subsoil; from the germination of the seed the roots adapt to withstand wind and weather. When the wolds were sheepwalks the vegetation consisted of more small herbs than grasses, and it was this mixture of

herbs and grasses combined with the rigour of a hill climate which bred the Cotswold breed of sheep whose wool was so valuable to England's economy in the
Middle Ages.

The wold landscape in the north is austere, bare ridge succeeding bare ridge in
subtle curving folds and the whole dominated by wide skies with an ever-changing
play of light and shade defeating monotony. An occasional rounded beech clump
planted by a nineteenth-century landowner to commemorate an important personal
or national event makes a dark focal point in the light tones of the wolds, a few
belts of wind-tattered conifers on the skyline introduce an alien fringe to the otherwise onward flow. Hill farms and buildings rarely interrupt the skyline. Built of
stone from a local quarry, sited in shallow folds for protection against the wind,
they blend into the scene and are a natural part of it. Indeed, such is the quality of
the weathered limestone that in misty weather buildings merge into the background
and seem as insubstantial as the mist itself.

The villages are mostly in the valleys or on the lower slopes beside the bright
streams and little rivers, and it is here one finds the elms and chestnuts, the orchard
trees and churchyard yews, a kindlier world sheltered by enfolding hillsides and
reached by winding byways branching from the main roads. Until the coming of
motor car, tractor and lorry they were remote in spirit if not in mileage from the
main commercial thoroughfares, and the old traditions lingered on until the
First World War eroded more by time than by outside influences. The war brought
a more intensive farming, an opening up of the hills to modern methods, the
ploughing of old pastures. The farming depressions of the 1930s, when many
farmers whose families had farmed Cotswold for generations were obliged to sell
their land, also helped in the decline of the traditional ways, but even the newcomers discovered that the normal laws of agriculture were not always applicable
to Cotswold—that in many instances old methods best suited the soil and the
climate. But the slumps and depressions also meant that the speculative builders
and the introduction of alien building materials they used in the mushroom growth
of new building elsewhere after the war found little opportunity on Cotswold.
There was little need for new houses on a big scale when younger people unable to
find a living on the land were seeking work elsewhere. The region sank again into a
rural backwater. This has been a recurring pattern down the ages. It happened when
Cotswold ceased to be one of the chief suppliers of wool in the Middle Ages, and
in the early years of the nineteenth century when the bulk of the clothing trade of
south Cotswold shifted to the north of England with the introduction of steam-
powered machinery. The small towns revived for a few years in the coaching era,
and being on through routes their inns provided hospitality for travellers and good

posting stations, but the coming of the railways extinguished that prosperity, without contributing anything in exchange. Most of the railway stations were situated well away from the towns and villages, landowners being prejudiced against railways at that time. Northleach, for instance, had no station within seven miles.

Today no sign of these depressing years remains. Since it has been designated as an area of outstanding natural beauty, not only are the authorities alert in its preservation but the inhabitants also maintain a watchful eye on the amenities. Newcomers, particularly, have an acute consciousness of their responsibilities and properties are cherished not only for their restored comeliness but because they have become a status symbol. Cotswold, therefore, has been reconstituted into an area not only tolerant of the ancient and picturesque but demanding it, sometimes to a point of over-emphasis. But enough of the original tradition remains to make the revival an awakening and not an entire remaking. The power of the local oolitic limestone to blend into the landscape, to weather harmoniously, to be in the right place wherever it is used works the magic.

# Cotswold Vernacular

AN irregular belt of limestone runs diagonally across England from Lyme Bay in Dorset to between Filey and Redcar on the east coast. This stone in the days when transport of heavy building material was difficult and expensive was the chief building material within and around this zone. As trade and the population began to increase in the second half of the seventeenth century, the western and eastern ends of this zone became more open to outside influences and after the Industrial Revolution, when houses for factory workers were needed in quantity, they were put up in the cheapest materials available without regard for taste or comeliness. The Cotswolds, however, being more remote and steeped in traditions of building going back to the masons who built the great religious houses of Gloucestershire, were not affected by outside influences. The masons continued to use local stone in a style best suited to the locality, the main features being steeply-pitched roofs covered with stone slates, gables and dormers, mullioned windows and massive chimney stacks. This style has been described as Gothic, Tudor, Elizabethan, but what H. J. Massingham called its 'medieval mannerisms' went on long after the Elizabethan period which inspired them.

It reached its greatest flowering between the last quarter of the sixteenth and the beginning of the eighteenth century but long after that time it continued to flourish, absorbing the classical revival and its several manifestations, the early Victorian and later Gothic revivals. Only the incidentals, the windows, porches and ornament, were changed to suit the period, and as it is the nature of oolitic limestone to take all styles to itself the unity remained for the most part unspoilt.

It is not easy to analyse why the overall appearance of a village, a terrace of cottages or an individual house is so pleasing, for the reasons are many and diverse; and even when they have been analysed an intangible essence remains unexplained. The proportions show that the masons followed definite rules, combining them with an uncanny sense of how to vary the details within the convention. There is the texture of the stone, which gives out as well as takes in a bloom of light and keeps a faint warmth of its original quarry colour after decades of weathering, and

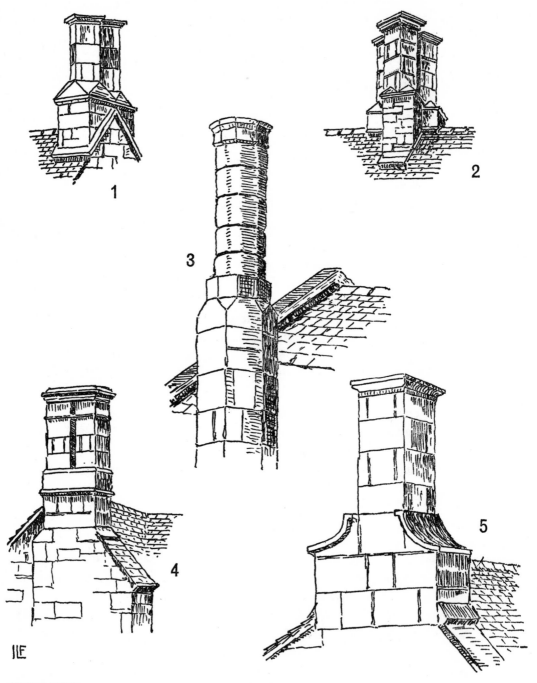

CHIMNEYS

*1, Haresfield. 2, Harescombe. 3, 5, Chipping Campden. 4, Stanway.*

there are the darker tones of the roof tiles, with a deep velvety finish of moss and lichen making a satisfactory climax to the whole. The stone is kindly and does not suggest heaviness, nor is there that sense of unwieldy bulk one finds in the stone-built areas of northern England, where the stone and not the mason is the master. Cotswold stone can be worked to precise measurements and dressed to a fine surface, and this is evident not only in important buildings but in the dressing of the doors and windows of the humblest cottage. The solid rectangular units of the basic structure are made more aspiring by pointed gables and dormers, the uprights of moulded mullions, the linear relief of drip moulding, while a carved label stop, a decorative bracket holding a projecting slab of stone to shelter a doorway, a finial at the apex of a gable are like small exclamations of pleasure at the end of a job well done.

One cannot fail to notice how this felicity of style, added to skilful siting as when a small terrace of cottages is fitted into a narrow shelf on a steep hillside, occurs not as an occasional exercise but over and over again throughout the region. There is only a difference of degree, not of pattern, between the cottage and the manor house; the same elements are there whatever the scale. At its most elaborate the building is based on a few characteristic features, at its plainest the effect is never bleak utility and has some small individual touch to give it grace.

Large mansions designed by world-famous architects and built of imported stone do not come into the Cotswold vernacular but belong to the country at large. When the stone was obtained from the estate quarries then it worked its usual magic, adding to the pomp and elegance its own benevolent bloom, as at Barnsley Park near Cirencester. Moreover, when local stone was used local quarrymen and masons also worked on the building and probably rejoiced to do so, for there is nothing a good craftsman enjoys more than participating in a big job he can point to afterwards with pride. In recent years when the fabric of several eighteenth-century mansions has been undergoing repair the marks of the original masons have come to light. A man working on such a restoration told me he had learned a lot from old masons' work he had uncovered. When I asked him if I might give his name and quote him he pointed to a mason's mark he had recently uncovered on a worn cornice. 'We don't know that chap's name. And there must have been hundreds like him doing good work. I like to think I'm one of 'em.'

The typical features of the vernacular make good sense for the climate, the terrain, the building material. The steep pitch of the roof is essential when stone slates are used, for the Cotswolds are subject to sudden violent rain storms and if a heavy volume of water was unable to run away quickly the slates would become saturated and damp penetrate the rooms below. The overlapping of slates, the

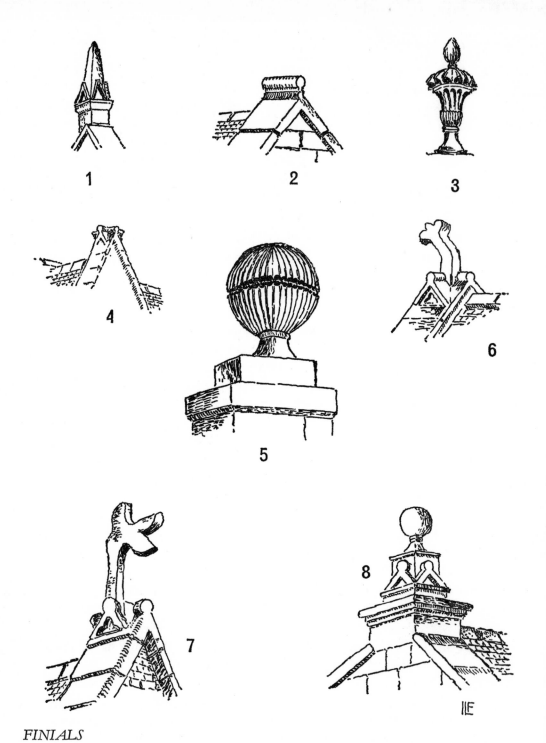

FINIALS

*1, 2, 4, 5, 8, Chipping Campden. 3, Mickleton. 6, Longborough. 7, Middle Littleton.*

packing of moss or hay under them and a roof-pitch of about 55 degrees ensured a watertight covering.

The gable was another distinctive feature in its several sizes and positions: to finish the end of a house where a chimney stack rises in diminishing courses; as a handsome chamber gable of two or three stories; a dormer in a cottage roof or a line of dormers in an otherwise flat-fronted terrace. Its position in the seventeenth century, when the parlour on one side of the central chimney stack was smaller than the principal living-room, was at the upper end over the living-room, but as merchants and yeomen became more prosperous a definite separation in living quarters between master and servants led to the parlour being enlarged, making both principal rooms and the gables over them of the same size. The addition of a projecting porch, a small room in itself with a loft above it having its own gable, produced a charming three-gabled frontage, 'the culmination and swan song of English medieval domestic architecture', to quote Hugh Braun, soon to be superseded in other parts of the country; but not on Cotswold, where the old tradition carried on.

Larger houses have their mullions divided by stone transoms, partly for strength and partly to break up the window space into standard-size units. The number of mullions diminished with each storey. A ground-floor window can have four to six lights with the central mullion more pronounced, the first floor three or four, the second two, and a third storey one light. A small window high under the end gable or, in a larger house, under each front gable, was often filled in with masonry during the time of the window tax. Dormers invariably have two lights.

Bay windows of flat projection are mostly the product of the early nineteenth century. Villages such as Chipping Campden and Broadway, consisting originally of one long street, show some charming examples of ground-floor bays with the bay combined with the front door under a single hood roofed with small stone slates, and the pattern can be seen also in small terraces of cottages, thus repeating the horizontal lines and darker tones of the roof, a device engaging in its simplicity and an indication that Cotswold traditions were not dead. In the days before village shops were purpose-built or large alterations to frontages were made for the display of goods, these bay-windowed cottages were often used for shops; indeed in some instances the bays may have been put in for that purpose, and there are many elderly people today who remember as children peering into the dim interior of such windows while trying to decide how to spend their pocket money.

The height of the walls of smaller houses and cottages was about fifteen feet, so that the upper storey was only about five feet or so at the eaves, leaving little room for windows. A solution was found by carrying the walls into miniature gables, or 'gablets', into which windows were inserted, letting air and light into the attics. When, late in the seventeenth century, the small house had become three-storeyed because of improvement in building techniques and because there was often not enough room to spread outwards in the narrow valleys, a line of dormers on an otherwise plain-fronted house became a useful as well as an architectural delight of the style.

A handyman could build the bulk of the fabric of a cottage, but masons were employed for the quoins, window and door dressings and chimneys. The earliest chimneys were built on to the end of the structure and were the most expensive part of the work, massive at the base and diminishing in stages, with a plain mould-ing marking each stage to keep the rain from saturating the stone. Later, when chimneys became general and more rooms in large houses had fireplaces, the pat-tern became a rectangular structure divided into two parts and separated by an internal stack ending in a chimney stack cluster, sometimes with the individual chimneys incorporated into a solid block above the roof and sometimes divided, the shape outlined with plain mouldings like miniature shelves. A typical feature of a small cottage with no fireplace in the upper room was the curve of the chimney breast ascending to the roof.

The fireplace in the living-room was the most important and ornamental feature of the house, its generous proportions giving an air of comfort as well as making a focal point. When work was done and all sat round to enjoy the warmth and peace at close of day it drew the occupants together in a sense of belonging so necessary to a contented existence. The usual width of the fireplace was about six feet, the height four to five feet, and the large flues tapered to the roof and were carried straight up so that it was possible to see the sky from below. It had stone jambs and an immense oak beam showing the rough cuts of the adze which formed it, but in houses where the owner had the means as well as the desire to enrich his domain the head could be of stone shaped as a flat four-centred arch, with the initials of himself and his wife, the date of building or coats of arms carved on the over-mantel.

On one or both sides of the fireplace inside the ingle a seat, just wide enough to sit on, was often placed in the thickness of the masonry with an arch above giving room for the head, a refuge in the daytime for an old man or woman from the busy-ness around them. They must have found it a smoky place but lack of draughts about their legs and the warmth compensated for this, and since wood was the customary fuel there would be no poisonous fumes. In any case soot and smoke were accepted as the inevitable accompaniment of fire. Small niches might be hollowed out to hold a cup or jar, or little cupboards fitted on either side for such things as salt and spices that it was necessary to keep dry. Old stone houses were damp and the conscientious housewife must have waged war for at least nine months of the year against damp and mildew.

## DOORHEADS AND PORCHES

By the beginning of the eighteenth century when the surge of new building was well under way the arched entrance with moulded jambs, frieze and cornice had become well established for the better class house, ranging from the manor house to those of the yeoman farmer, merchants and prosperous tradesmen. It was a period when a new middle class was rapidly emerging, a class that was alive to the necessity of equipping itself with the trappings of wealth and success if it was to rise still higher in the social scale. The small cottages of the farm labourers had plain lintels of wood or stone, sometimes with a row of stone slates projecting over the door to provide a little shelter, the door being the only entrance to the cottage and opening directly into the living-room. When a family rose out of the labouring classes, if only by a step or two, a more elaborate doorway was often an indication of the new status, gratifying an instinct strong in a Cotsaller to add a distinctive touch to his dwelling.

The door-hood took many forms, from the heavy slab of stone supported by carved stone brackets to the sharp-pointed arch like a miniature roof ridge decorated with heavy mouldings and raised on an elaborately convoluted console bracket. The variety within the convention challenged the mason's inventiveness and one can see how often he departed from the pattern book, making his own design.

The drip course followed the same pattern as the moulding over windows and terminated at the jambs with horizontal or dropped ends, and it was in the label stops that the carver found scope for his imagination. A building such as a school or one with ecclesiastical associations was sometimes finished with sculptured heads, but usually the label stops were based on the diamond or boss surrounded by a square formed of the same type of moulding as was used for the drip course. The drip course also framed the arched heads of two-, three- or four-centred stones according to the period of the structure, the most common in the late medieval period being the four-centred form of one stone steep in outline at first, but the arch becoming flatter in later examples.

Towards the end of the eighteenth century designs merged into an awareness of the Renaissance and doorheads and porches were often the first intimation that the new fashion had reached Cotswold. The front of many an Elizabethan manor house, for instance, was given the new look by a porch of classical design. It is the

**DOORHEADS**

*1, 2, 4, 5, Chipping Campden. 3, South Cerney.*

earliest of these, before the style became pompous, which achieve the greatest elegance and charm, kept in bounds by a certain austerity of line and ornament. Today time has weathered them into an intrinsic adornment of the whole building. There is a certain reticence in a Cotswold building as there is in a Cotswold landscape and the old craftsmen were instinctively aware of this and never overloaded their work with ornament.

# Urban Vernacular

FROM the days of the medieval woolmen until the decay of the clothing trade in South Cotswold in the first half of the nineteenth century the small market towns were concerned with industry whose products went far beyond local requirements. Cirencester, Chipping Campden, Tetbury, Northleach, were centres where raw wool and fleeces, after being collected from the neighbouring sheep farms, were bought and sold by factors and merchants and then sent to London and the Low Countries. Storage was usually under the same roof as the merchant's dwelling house. As the trade increased and there was no more space to extend lengthwise along the street, wings were added to the original building at right-angles to the frontage, thus forming a courtyard or courtyards with offices and store rooms on each side. Where this was insufficient, separate warehouses were sometimes erected. Northleach still keeps such a warehouse, now an antique shop, on the left as one comes into the village from Cheltenham direction, though it was refaced during the early nineteenth century. On the right of Chalford High Street, Thanet Cottage, with two-light mullioned and transomed windows and continuous dripmoulds, was once a clothier's warehouse of four storeys.

A way had to be made to take laden packhorses into the courtyard to load and unload, and in many instances this is the reason for the archways which are such a picturesque feature of Campden and Burford. Ancient inns also had these entrances but these were of wider span to admit waggons and coaches and usually of a later date. The bulk of wool and fleeces were carried in packhorse trains.

These entrances were erected in Cotswold style with stone jambs and moulded arches, and when the merchants, because of their contacts with London and the Continent, succumbed to the influence of the Classical Revival and changed the façades of their houses, the archways were left unaltered and added to the mixture of styles which makes the architectural history of a Cotswold street so fascinating to unravel. By the time wool ceased to be exported to the Low Countries the cloth mills and their buildings developed their own urban vernacular. Northleach, Campden, Cirencester, however, without the water power necessary for large-scale cloth-making, stayed more or less moribund, decreasing in population and importance until the beginning of the twentieth century, their late medieval style never overwhelmed by the fashions of the next two centuries.

Urban vernacular, except in Cirencester and the Golden Valley, lacks the grace of its rural counterpart, though the excellence of the mason's craft can be seen in the fabric of dressed stone. The prosperity of Cirencester in the years when the style reached its finest quality can be seen in the narrow streets leading off the Market Place. Dollar Street, Thomas Street and Coxwell Street still keep many of their original houses (Pls 12–16). To quote David Verey's *Cotswolds* in 'The Buildings of England' series: 'There is more genuine survival here than in any other town in the Cotswolds'. In Coxwell Street one sees a continuous range.

The cloth trade was responsible for much building and rebuilding in the south of the region until the trade declined in the first half of the nineteenth century, Stroud alone going over to steam power and competing with the industrial centres of the north. Where the mills were built on streams outside the villages clothiers provided accommodation for their workers near the mills where their own houses were situated. In many instances the mill and domestic premises were under the same roof. The Golden Valley along the Frome has many examples dating from the seventeenth century onwards and erected by local masons using local stone in true Cotswold style. Near Chalford parish church the Bliss Mills and Valley Works have a fine pair of gate piers with ball finials, once the entrance to an old mill; Valley House has a gabled front and mullioned windows with arched lights; Greystones, of later date with nineteenth-century additions, one end used for manufacture the other as domestic quarters, with mullioned windows. These are only a few of the old mills and mill-owners' houses now modernized into handsome residences in this district. The Cotswold style was still part of the mason's tradition late into the nineteenth century, as many a later mill and house shows, the mill buildings having mullioned windows and arched doorways on the lower floors. These buildings had to expand upwards, for the narrow valleys left little room for expansion on the ground, while the weavers' cottages dotted the hillsides above wherever a shelf of flat ground offered a perching place and a spring of water for soaking the yarn. This is very noticeable above Chalford, where the cottages are reached by steep narrow winding lanes, once packhorse trails when the trade was flourishing, and a source of much annoyance to the clothiers' wives when they were able to afford carriages, the horses finding the roads too steep and narrow for safety.

Light was essential to the weaver and consequently the windows of his cottage were made larger than the traditional size and usually without drip mouldings or mullions (Pls 27–8). Favoured sites were southern slopes where the sun provided warmth as well as light, for the weaver—unlike the shearers, tenters, fullers and dyers who processed the cloth—often lived miles from the mill and the fortnightly walk to take the newly-woven length to the mill was one of the rituals of a weaver's life, the day when he put on his best suit of broadcloth and was released from his long daily stint at the loom.

The tall, rather gaunt town house of three storeys, its façade relieved only by a row of dormers in the high attics and a flight of steps leading to the front door, is a type of urban vernacular that probably owes its height to the building regulations of medieval times when land within the perimeter of the town's protecting walls was scarce and citizens' houses were restricted to less than twenty feet frontage, with courtyards behind where store-rooms and domestic outbuildings were situated. As time went on, when more living accommodation was required building upward was the only solution. Refacing of the walls and enlargement of the windows in the nineteenth century often did away with the traditional mullions and mouldings, and there were some houses built just after the Civil War when plainness in building, as well as in dress and religion, was the official fashion.

# Farmhouses

BEFORE the Enclosures, when holdings of agricultural land were scattered in strips in great common fields and no farmer could call any particular strip his own, the house of the yeomen farmer was situated amongst the dwellings and workshops of blacksmith, carpenter, tailor and all the other people who made up the village community. Isolated farmhouses, though generally built in the vernacular, date mostly from Georgian days and were erected when it had become possible for a farmer to live on his own land in the midst of his own fields. The exceptions are medieval manor houses, which can be distinguished by remains of the original fabric and lay-out, and small holdings reclaimed from waste land by some enterprising squatter well away from the village.

Until the beginning of the twentieth century many farmhouses still continued to function in the heart of a village, particularly those consisting of one long street running through a narrow valley with fields rising to the hills behind the gardens, paddocks and yards of the houses and cottages. Ebrington, near Chipping Campden, for instance, has several farms with their rickyards, cattle sheds and other buildings facing the village street (Pls 29, 30), though with one exception these are mainly nineteenth century and later, probably because of rebuilding.

A noticeable aspect of an early farmhouse is its length; even when built a century later it kept the pattern of the seventeenth-century Long House with living and working accommodation under one roof. A typical example seen today in practically every Cotswold village is of two storeys with a two- or three-gabled front, attic windows under the gables, and at each end lower structures built for oxen, farm implements, cider house, dairies and workshops.

The main kitchen-living-room was on one side of the front door with a smaller room, the parlour, on the other side. It is interesting that in the earliest examples there was only one front door despite the length, with a wide opening at one side leading into the back premises and yards. When the farmers moved out to new houses on their own land these spaces were often filled in by new houses facing the street, and this is one of the reasons for the tall narrow houses one finds in small towns and villages.

In the larger farmhouses there could be a dining parlour as well as the little parlour on the other side of the front door, though this refinement was more often added in the eighteenth century. Before that time and on farms with a working farmer the workers ate with the family in the kitchen, with the farmer at the head of the table and the others in their order of importance ranged below him. The rest of the ground floor was for storage, cheese rooms, granary and implements, for in those days the farmer kept his corn, tackle, and often his best animals under one roof.

The staircase in the middle of the house ended directly into the main bedroom where the master and his wife slept, and everyone had to pass through this room to reach their own sleeping quarters, women on one side, men on the other, with members of the family nearest the master. When the difference in status between masters and servants became more outwardly pronounced and 'the itching anxiety of the upper and middling classes'—to quote G. M. Trevelyan—'was to teach the ground law of subordination to the inferior orders', a back staircase was inserted and the main stairs kept for family use.

'Outshots' or 'talluts', single-storey additions above a lean-to, were ranged at right angles to the main block when it was no longer possible to expand length-wise and these made cart sheds and shelters for cattle, and stables when horses re-placed oxen. Later, by raising the outshot to the height of the original building, a double-span house evolved with a pair of single-span roofs. The necessity of keep-ing the valley between the two roofs from becoming water-logged when stone slates were the roofing material called for much skill by the tiler, and renovations of such houses in recent years usually do away with the valleys and put the two parts under one roof span.

After the Enclosures and re-allotment of land, when the farmers moved to new farmhouses outside the village street, the old farmhouses went through many vicissitudes. Some were split up into labourers' tenements in the bad years of the late nineteenth century, others became inns, and they were well suited for this because of their entrances for carts and horses: in Broadway one even became a workhouse. Today many of those still remaining have been reconditioned and modernized into comely residences or establishments where antiques are sold, their vernacular features lovingly cherished. They are eagerly sought after by wealthy commuters or retired people and when one comes on to the market it fetches a high price.

The last half of the eighteenth century was a period of great expansion for the rural middle class who were rapidly becoming gentleman farmers, and this meant their domain must express their rising prosperity and importance. The local master builders were mainly responsible, men brought up in the old traditions but who were aware of the Renaissance and could embellish an old house or build a new one in that style. But while over the rest of England the eighteenth-century farmhouse was developing into a square type of building, for the most part the Cotswold builders still kept to the single-span building having a definitely long axis. Extra accommodation was provided by wings at right angles, thus forming an L-shaped or E-shaped complex and providing a courtyard or courtyards at the back. Except for a wide entrance for waggons and cattle at one end the courtyards were completely enclosed, a safety as well as a sheltering device, shelter being essential on hill farms where the wind blows cold and snow drifts high in winter. On more important farms the way to the yards was through a wide stone archway and, keeping to medieval fashion, some of these gateways had rooms above, as at Baunton Manor Farm near Cirencester.

By the time many ancient families of Norman origin, families who had farmed the manors in their own right or as tenants of a religious house, had died out or were impoverished, a new kind of squire had emerged whose ancestors had acquired land by easy purchase of monastic estates after the Dissolution. Enclosures helped to increase their acreage as land became available from yeoman farmers and small holders obliged to sell because they were unable to afford the cost of fencing their fields, and changes from subsistence farming to farming for profit brought them greater prosperity, especially those who could now farm on a big scale. Labour was cheap and plentiful, for those men obliged to sell their land went to swell the ranks of those seeking employment. Moreover, many gentlemen farmers had interests in the cloth trade and the expanding commerce overseas. Some had started as clothiers, bought an estate out of the profits and then given up industry to become country gentlemen. The reign of the feudal barons and the powerful abbots and priors had long ago come to an end, and as Justices of the Peace for the Crown eighteenth- and nineteenth-century gentlemen farmers acquired official as well as local authority. Naturally they wanted to stress their dignity by the manner of house in which they lived and by the buildings of their estate. Everything from the house itself to the humblest outhouse had to be of good design and workmanship, and it was a period when these things were understood not only by the experts but by every landowner.

Letters, diaries and other records of the time and the historians who interpret them enumerate the faults of this middle-class society, their greed for more land, their overbearing behaviour to those they considered their inferiors, their determination to keep what they had and get what they could, and they probably deserved these descriptions, but one must also remember that they enriched the Cotswold landscape with felicitous groups of farms and farm buildings, planted the beech clumps and beech avenues we have come to regard as characteristic of Cotswold and were the pioneers of a more productive agriculture.

# Cottages

APART from the tied cottages belonging to the farm or estate occupied by workers concerned in the daily tasks of the farm there were the cottages mainly occupied by the tradesmen of the village, the blacksmith, tailor, baker, carpenter, cobbler and others who were necessary to the community but who were not bound closely to a single farmer and who had more freedom of movement. These cottages were often held on a three-life system, the landlord providing the site and the materials, and the tenant the labour. The tenant, his son and grandson lived in it rent free for their lifetimes, and afterwards it reverted to the landlord. Both these systems of tenure were the cause of much hardship when farms changed hands or the original landlords of the three-life system sold their land. In Sapperton in 1912 there was still a cottage held rent free under this arrangement, and in most villages until recently one could find old people living in cottages rent free and unaware of the real owners of the property. One cottage I was told about could be tenanted by anyone who could procure the key from a former occupier. As few repairs were ever made to this kind of cottage, and it had no modern conveniences and was generally damp and unhygienic, in recent years the local health and sanitary authorities arranged that when the aged tenant died or was carted off to a home or hospital the cottage was scheduled for demolition. Most of them were too far gone to repair.

The accommodation of these old cottages usually consisted of one kitchen-living-room and a combined larder and store room on the ground floor, with a landing and bedroom leading from it above, the landing being used as another bedroom. The living-room had a large open fireplace and some had a bread oven opening into it and forming a semi-circular projection outside. Some cottages were built with drystone walls and pointed with mortar made of lime, dried horse and cow dung collected from the gullies in the road. Floors were generally covered with squared stone flags from the quarry laid directly on the earth.

Sometimes the bread oven was situated in a back kitchen, a small offshut added to the storeroom behind the kitchen (Pls 63, 64). The oven was heated by bundles of faggotts thrust into the interior, and when the faggotts had burned away the ashes were removed by brushing with a bundle of twigs or a goose's wing. After the bread was baked enough heat remained in the oven to cook cakes and pies. Baking day began with the making of the bread in the kitchen, followed by cake and pie-making while the bread was rising in the large yellow crock covered with a cloth before the kitchen fire. It was hard and tiring work, particularly kneeding a week's bread for a large family, but most housewives considered it the most satisfactory day's work of the week. As one old lady said to me, 'There was something to show for it, and it put everyone into a good temper coming into the kitchen and smelling the baking'. Her mother used to bake on Friday after the house had been cleaned down, and this was the day the children ran home quickly from school instead of dawdling to play, because their mother baked them a flat bread cake, sometimes with currants and lard in it, as a special treat for their tea, she told me.

Mrs Radburn of Broadwell described to me how her grandmother, who lived in a cottage with no means of cooking except an open fire, used to bake a cake in an old blackened crock turned upside down over the dough on the hearth with hot ashes heaped over it until it was cooked. 'We kids loved the crusty outside. Sometimes it was burnt black and there were always little crumbs of cinders in it but we ate cinders and all and enjoyed it.' This same grandmother would cook a whole Sunday dinner in an iron pot over the fire. First the meat was put in and then at intervals according to the cooking time required the vegetables in nets, with a plum duff in a calico bag on top of the lot. The skill needed for this form of cooking was in keeping the fire well under control. George Swinford's museum at Filkins has sets of nets used by cottage women for this purpose when he was a boy.

Sunday roasts could also be cooked at the baker's for a copper or two. When he had taken out the bread there was sufficient heat to cook the dinners of the village, and Mrs Elliot told me that when she was a girl it was her job to fetch the dinner on Sunday, having first warned her father at the pub that dinner would soon be ready. There would be a long line of children waiting in the baker's yard and she remembered it vividly because the bigger boys teased the girls as they waited their turn, but once started on the way home there was no more rough play, a Sunday dinner being too precious to run any risks of its coming to harm; even the most mischievous boys recognized this fact.

During the late eighteenth and the nineteenth centuries those landowners wanting to improve the appearance of their estates and the comfort of their workpeople built sets of new cottages, but the designs were usually commissioned from an architect and, though built by local builders and from stone from the estate quarries, the cottages were often subject to the whims and ideas of the landowners and their wives, who had notions about the picturesque which had little to do with the traditional building style of the region. A good example of a simple effective design was a semi-circular terrace of four cottages, known as Half Moon Cottages, erected by John Chamberlayne of Maugersbury near Stow-on-the-Wold in 1800 (Pl. 23). In most instances the earlier estate cottages show a better taste than those erected in the nineteenth century.

Each of the Half Moon Cottages had an acre of land, with a pig-sty and a spring of fresh water nearby. The lower room was twelve feet square and there were two bedrooms eight by twelve feet each, a generous size and height in those days, and there was another room above the bedrooms capable of holding beds and lit by a skylight. A communal washhouse, bakehouse and schoolroom was provided in the centre of the building. The half circle of the complete block is repeated in the arches over windows and doors, with a small circular window at each end. The cottages have now been modernized and embellished into a single residence.

# Tithe Barns

VERY few of the farmhouses and their buildings once occupied by farmers whose landlords were the abbots and priors of the monasteries and abbeys exist today in their entirety, but there is one valuable building which has survived unchanged on many farms, the great tithe barn to which the wool, fleeces and corn due to the monks were brought to be stored from the surrounding countryside each harvest. Cotswold is rich in great barns and the greatest of these are the tithe barns. They were placed apart from the main working area of the yards but within their shelter, if possible on slightly rising ground, and were the most impressive of all the farm buildings. At sheep-sheering and harvest the stewards from the monasteries, sometimes the abbots themselves, would journey from manor to manor supervising the gathering of the crops and watching to see their share safely stowed away. Judging by the size of the barns their share must have been considerable. At a time when most farmers still farmed at subsistence levels the religious houses, after taking what they wanted for their own use, sold the remaining produce, the sale of wool particularly making a substantial part of their income.

Tithe barns taken over by the new lords of the manor after the fall of the monasteries continued in use down the centuries. First oxen and then horses pulled the high-loaded waggons through the wide, high cart porches into the vast interior, and then tractors replaced the horses and threshing machines the men with the flails on the barn floor. Barns were used for threshing until the end of the nineteenth century, the ears winnowed by the natural draught between the doors or from primitive winnowing machines. Now combine harvesters and corn driers have taken over on the arable farms but the barns still have their uses, their interiors portioned off to house calves or to provide stabling for horses kept for pleasure as well as occasional light work. They are used for storage of all kinds including those thousand and one small things from a piece of old chain to a hoard of sacks which a farmer finds difficult to get rid of because they may be useful one day. Farmers are notorious hoarders, and always have been, and they found it necessary in the days when bad roads and poor transport isolated them from shopping centres. We should be thankful for this today; most farms which have been in existence over a hundred years are fruitful depositories of bygones, valuable today as farm history.

Small wonder the tithe barns have lasted for the past five or six hundred years. As the Church's treasure houses on earth they were built to withstand time, weather and predators. Those which have perished have fallen by man's hand, not by the wear of centuries. A number disappeared at the turn of the century when farming was in a bad way and the ancient stone slates on their roofs were more valuable than the buildings themselves. Roofs were stripped and the slates sold for a good price, thousands going to America; the walls and interiors, left exposed to the ravages of weather and anyone wanting cheap building stone, gradually became ruined shells to be cleared away later to make room for dutch barns, silage towers or milking parlours.

The tithe barn at Frocester, below Stroud, erected for the Abbot de Gamage between 1264 and 1306, which once served for the collection of tithes of the Benedictine monastery, is a typical example of the many to be found on Cotswold. Others differ only in small detail of shape of window or in the build-up of the roof timbers. The barn at Postlip near Winchcombe, for instance, has its cruck-trusses set in low stone plinths; the majority, however, have their principals built into the walls and with the aid of massive stone buttresses outside support the enormous weight of the stone-tiled roof.

Frocester barn measures 184 feet long, 30 feet wide, and is 36 feet high to the roof ridge. The walls are 12 feet high where they meet the eaves, which gives an indication of the steep pitch of the roof, whose immense span is covered with heavy stone slates stained with the accretions of mosses and lichens over the past 600 years. There are twelve bays inside, divided by principals fourteen to sixteen feet apart. It has two cart porches wide and high enough to take a loaded waggon with room to spare on each side. When I looked inside a few years ago, sniffing the dusty barn smell of hay and straw, several men unloading a trailer looked like dwarfs in its dim interior. The structure has been well preserved and is in good condition; it looks as if it will last another 600 years.

Stanway's tithe barn was built for the Abbot of Tewkesbury in the fourteenth century and came into possession of the Traceys of Toddington when they took over the manor after the Dissolution. It is built of local stone, the slates from the Buckle Street quarries nearby. The roof is supported on cruck frames bedded in the walls, the collars reinforced by curved braces and two-tiered wind-braces, a beautiful example of roof timbering toughened by age to an adamantine hardness. It has a gabled porch, and a scratch dial on the inner face of the jamb of a small doorway suggests the use of stone taken from an earlier building belonging to the abbey. It has always been the custom on Cotswold to use ruins as quarries. Carved stones of Saxon origin have been found in the fabric of Norman churches with the carving hidden from view, and at every large-scale restoration vestiges of earlier building are revealed.

For the most part the medieval masons kept the structure of a barn severely plain, the long base, the steep-pitched roofs, the cart porches sometimes gabled but usually with a wooden lintel. The workmanship and skill of the builders is seen in the good quality of the masonry and the roof timbers. At Syde, a tiny village off Ermin Street a few miles before it comes to the top of Birdlip, the tithe barn has two medieval traceried windows on the west side, each being of two lights, and it has been suggested that part might have served as a priest's house and so received this small adornment. Hampnett, in the heart of the old sheepwalks where Will Midwinter, the factor of Northleach, obtained wool and fleeces for the Cely family, has a massive barn dominating a group of barns and farm buildings placed close together, all of them larger than the church nearby, and emphasizing how these wide lonely uplands must have produced large crops of wool and corn during the medieval period until the late nineteenth century. Though these products are now dealt with by different methods the barns themselves are evidence of a continuity of purpose for hundreds of years, and evidence of the bounty and fertility of the hills.

# Barns and Granaries

IF one were unaware of the importance of homegrown oats, barley and wheat before the general imports of grain from the prairies it could be deduced from the size and number of barns and granaries on every good-sized hill farm, and from the fact that no new stone barns were built after the last years of the nineteenth century when corn had ceased to be economic to produce. Before the Enclosures the corn grown was mainly for consumption by the farmer, his family and his workers, and one season's harvest had to last the year through as well as provide seed for the next year's crop. This meant plenty of storage space, but the greater number of barns were built when arable succeeded the sheep-walks and the new landowners of the vast enclosed fields began to grow corn on a big scale and erected the barns as part of their handsome farm buildings, not only for storage but to enhance their estates.

Oats were a vital source of food for animals as well as humans, straw was essential for bedding and a source of manure to fertilize the fields, artificial fertilizers being practically unknown, and the amount to be stored necessitated the provision of store houses on an appropriate scale. The introduction of root crops and green feeding stuffs in the eighteenth century expanded the farm's potential without reducing the need for storage space. William Marshall commented on this:

'The size of the barns in this country is above par. On height above anything I have observed, 52 by 20 feet to the plate, is esteemed a good barn. This size admits of four bays of 10 feet each, with a floor in the middle. And of threshing floors 12 by 14 to 18 by 20 feet. The best of oak but some of stone. But a species of earthen floor which is thought to be superior to floors of stone or any other material except sound oak.'

He goes on about their construction, the materials differing slightly from Rudge's later description of 'Grip': '. . . . of local stone brash and gravel and beaten with a flat wooden beetle until the surface becomes as hard as stone and rings at every stroke like metal. If properly made they are said to last a length of years: being equally proof against the flail and the broom.'

The decline of the barn as the most important building on the farm came about the beginning of the twentieth century, when it was no longer profitable to grow corn on the great upland fields, and although the majority of Cotswold farmers with characteristic stubbornness and their long tradition of arable and sheep farming refused to believe the changes had come to stay, there began a grim period when because of lack of profits comeliness gave way to makeshift as buildings needing repair were patched up as cheaply as possible or allowed to fall into decay. When farming climbed out of these depressions and began to pay again during and after the last war new methods had made barns and granaries obsolete. Today some are being transformed into handsome residences, oddly enough resembling in their shape the Long Houses of the seventeenth century belonging to the heyday of the Cotswold vernacular.

The buildings for housing oxen and the teams of horses which succeeded them, the cows for milk and cheese, were generally contained in the wings of the farm-house, but the barns stood alone, often placed so that they helped to enclose a cow- or sheep-fold. The design of the barn was governed by its principal use, its wide doors and porches opposite each other in the centre of the length dividing it into portions, one side for stacking the sheaves and the place for the threshed straw on the other, with a threshing floor between them where in the winter months hand threshing was carried on. The small barns had three bays some 16 feet across. All had double doors.

A smooth floor was essential if the grain was not to be bruised. Rudge describes a floor called 'Grip', common in farmhouse kitchens as well as outbuildings, a composition of lime and ashes laid in a moist state to the thickness of four to five inches and rammed with a heavy wooden slab to hardness and a smooth surface. In his opinion this was not a good flooring for barns because it bruised the grain, particularly wheat, and he added that when oak could be procured it gave the grain 'a smooth and shining face'. Oak, however, except in that part of Cotswold near the Forest of Dean, was expensive and difficult to procure and other woods such as elm and poplar were often substituted.

The usual flooring put down in farmhouse kitchens, dairies, cheese-rooms and brewhouses was of thin slabs of blue lias found with the oolitic limestones in local quarries, but this was unsuitable for barns for it has a tendency to flake, the flakes disintegrating when damp into a soft fine powder, and the essential condition for a threshing floor was a dust-free surface. There was a boarded division at the end of the threshing floor where the grain was placed before it was winnowed and ready to be stored in the granary.

The barns belonging to the farmstead differed from the tithe barn in their windows or ventilation holes. The tithe barn had long narrow slits widening as they went inward through the thick walls, the farm barn's ventilation holes could be circular, oval or triangular, sometimes with sills or narrow ledges underneath so that owls hunting mice could alight there before they entered. On a manorial farm rows of nest holes for pigeons were sometimes placed under the end gable with the floor of the pigeon loft boarded so that the birds could only enter by the holes provided for them (Pls 43, 44).

Granaries were purpose-built and were often separate buildings to keep them free from the rats and mice who had runs from one attached outbuilding to another through the rubble within the stone facing of the walls. These separate granaries were often built not only for use but to enhance the look of the farm, some with a touch of elegance befitting their importance. They were raised from the ground to eliminate damp, stored grain's greatest hazard, and were often put on stone staddles, those mushroom-like shapes on triangular bases now used as garden ornaments. The reason for the overhung mushroom-like heads was to make it impossible for vermin to climb up and reach the granary floor.

Another practice was to place a granary above an open cart-porch or stable with a flight of external steps leading up to it. The floor was boarded and the walls and ceilings plastered or smoothed to reduce spoilage by rats and mice and to keep it clean. The problem of the support of the granary walls was solved by the use of stone pillars together with lintels and arches, and these piers were rounded again to defeat vermin and to provide the largest possible opening and yet make the structure strong enough to support the weight above. Sometimes the pillars were of stout timber set in heavy stone plinths with moulded overhang, and the added refinement of turned columns, like gigantic chair legs.

When a granary was above a stable various ingenious trap-door devices were introduced to let down corn into the mangers, and it was not unknown for carters to make their own secret holes so that their horses received more than their official ration.

The occasional small traceried windows found in farm buildings like those at Broad Campden, Aldsworth, and Duntisbourne Leer probably came from the ruins of a monastery or ancient church and taken by the farmer to save the ancient fragment, because it was easier to insert a ready-made window opening than to make a new one, or to enhance his farm. This, of course, does not apply to those farm buildings taken over at the Dissolution and not destroyed because of their usefulness to the new owner.

# FARM SKILLS AND VILLAGE CRAFTS

*'Countrymen not yet cramped to the service of machines
were craftsmen and creators at will.'*

43. *Columbarium on great barn, Southrop.*

44. *Dovecot barn, Street Farm, Nympsfield.*

45. *Great Barn with dovecot and uncommon entrance, Winchcombe.*

46. *Tithe barn converted to a modern residence.*

47. *Granary at Court Farm, Nympsfield.*

48. *'Ventilators' in barn wall, Weston Subedge.*

49. *Buttressed barn-end, Didmarton.*

50. *'Tallut' at Stringer's Farm, Rodborough.*

51. *Stable at Southrop Manor; possibly of monastic origin.*

52. *'Necessary house', Frampton Mansell.*

53. *Field pump at Condi-cote.*

54. *Domestic pump at Old Court Farm, Lower Stone.*

55. *Pump in cottage garden, Ebrington. It formerly served a terrace of three cottages.*

56. *Fireplace in the Ebrington Arms, originally a
seventeenth-century farm-
house.*

57. *Range in cottage kitchen, Ebrington, still in use.*    58. *Kitchen range at Oakridge, put in about 1900.*

59. *Clockwork roasting-jack used at Quenington.*

60. *Chimney-jack, Quenington*
*(here hanging upside down).*

61. *Pastry cutter from The Grove, Wick Street, now at Wades Farm, Slad Valley.*
62. *Bread-oven peel, Woodford Green Farm, Berkeley.*

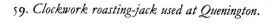

63. *Bread oven, Rodborough.*

64. *Bread oven, Southrop.*

65. *Cast-iron portable boiler used at Quenington.*

66. *Potato planter, Leonard Stanley.*

67. *Ferret box, Quenington.*

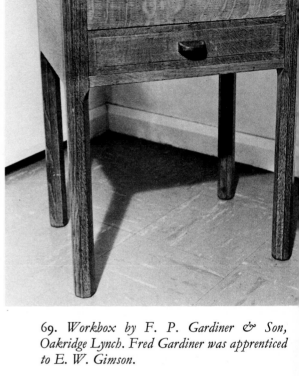

COTSWOLD REVIVAL. 68. *Painted wooden chest by Peter Waals. Metal-work by F. Baldwin, painting by Alfred and Louise Powell. Specially made for Rodmarton Manor by local craftsmen.*

69. *Workbox by F. P. Gardiner & Son, Oakridge Lynch. Fred Gardiner was apprenticed to E. W. Gimson.*

70. *Child's rush-seated chair, of 'Clissett' design; Rodmarton Manor.*

71. *Rush-seated chair by H. Davol; Rodmarton Manor.*

72. *Child's punishment chair; Rodmarton Manor.*

73–74. *Oak chest and chest of drawers by Peter Waals; Rodmarton Manor.*

75. *Yoke now at Priory Farm, Leonard Stanley; from Far Oakridge.*

76. *Wood and brass milk tub, various dairy implements. Old Court Farm, Lower Stone.*

77. *Hand-press for removing water from butter. Old Court Farm.*

78. *Butter-prints, Old Court Farm.*

79–80. *Butter-pat and butter-cup; Old Court Farm.*

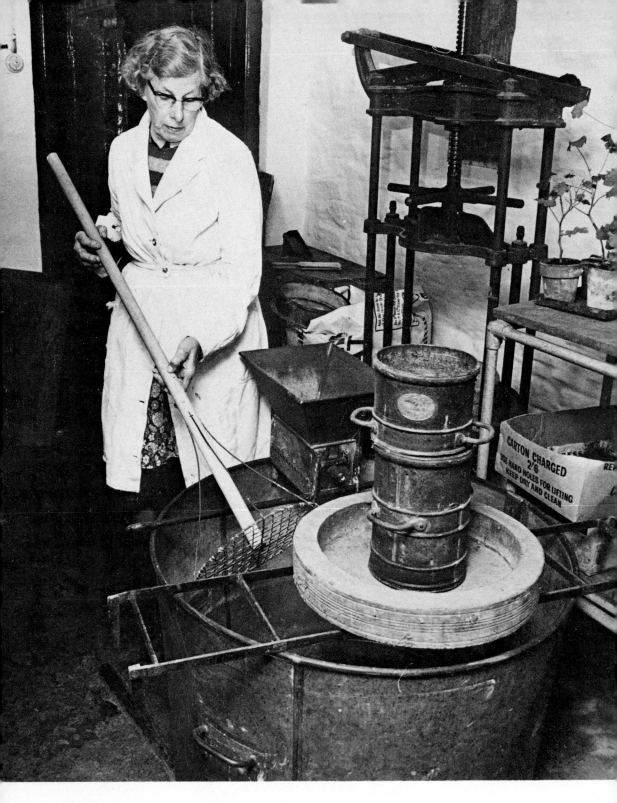

81. *Miss Victoria Smith, Old Court Farm, Lower Stone, probably the last practising cheese-maker. Curd-tub with curd-mill, wooden Double Gloucester vat; cheese press in background.*

82. *The louvred windows of the cheese house, Woodford Green Farm, Berkeley.*

83. *Cheese curd-breaker, Old Court Farm.*

84. *Cheese-room at Almsbury Farm, Winchcombe.*

85. *Cheese-house, Priory Farm, Leonard Stanley.*

# Furniture and Fittings

FARMHOUSE furnishings changed little from Elizabethan times until well into the eighteenth century. As elder son succeeded father the basic furniture remained in the house. The dresser, its lower part a long narrow table with two drawers or cupboards, two turned legs in front, the back resting not on legs but on a heavy piece of wood fixed to the wall to keep it steady, with shelves above displaying the crockery, was the most ornamental piece. The long table was large enough to seat the farmer, his family and the farm servants and its lower rail was usually scarred with the friction of hobnailed boots and the restless feet of children. The joint stool for carving, two wooden armchairs having plain railed backs or the more elaborate wheelback, the tall clock in its oak case in a corner, the oak settle (or of deal in some cottages), which in winter was drawn at right angles to the fire to keep out the draughts, made up the rest of the furniture. A cottage might have a chest of drawers where clothes were kept. About the hearth would be the crane for cooking pot and kettle, spits and hooks and tongs (Pl. 56), the bellows, while on the wall and in the recesses of the fireplace hung implements in daily use, the chopper, toasting forks, strainers and skimmers, the pig balance, and such things as bridle bits, whips, and other small things belonging to the farmer.

It would have been impossible for the furniture to be taken away unless in pieces, for the doors and windows were too small: it had been put together *in situ* by the local carpenter or builder, assembly units not being the modern innovation makers imply.

As the methods of cooking changed, a cooking range was inserted in the recess, or an oven on one side (Pls 57, 58), and up to the end of the nineteenth century it was not difficult to find a farmhouse fireplace whose later alterations and additions down the years could be removed layer by layer until the great wide arched recess of its first fireplace was revealed.

Upstairs the furniture was also basic, consisting of beds, a linen press, a cradle for the baby. The bed of the master and mistress would be solid, of oak or painted wood with panels and mouldings, in a prosperous farmhouse the best bed would

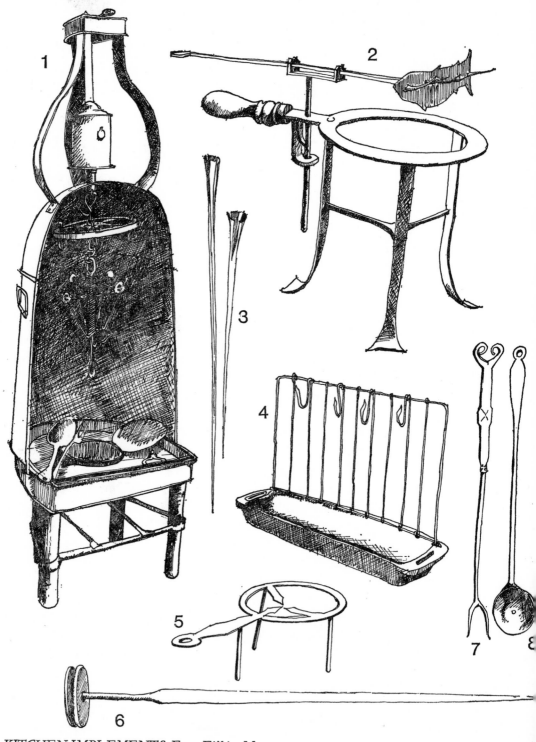

KITCHEN IMPLEMENTS. *From Filkins Museum*

*1. Dutch oven with jack and accessories. This was placed in front of a glowing fire; the clockwork jack turned the roast to cook it on all sides, and the fat and juices collected in the pan below. 2, Herring toaster. 3, Larding needles. 4, Lark spit, 6 inches long. 5, Trivet. 6, Spit. 7,8, Fork and ladle.*

be a four-poster with curtains and valance. I once watched a four-poster being taken to pieces because it was impossible to get it out of the bedroom other-wise, and as it was taken apart I saw that each piece was marked with pairs of notches as a guide to its original erection, and there was no metal in the whole construction.

The older linen chests were small and made of plain oak boards, while later ones had elaborately carved panels and moulded fronts and ends with a small receptacle inside a few inches deep to keep buttons, thread and mending material apart from the bulk of the contents. These chests and the old oak bible boxes eagerly sought by collectors had practically disappeared from the ordinary farmhouse by the turn of the century, but where an old farmhouse is no longer occupied by a farmer but taken over and modernized into a handsome country residence some of the old type of furniture has returned to it. This has been bought from antique dealers as expensive period pieces and now cherished not merely as useful articles of furniture but as valuable antiques.

Not all the oak presses, the carved chairs and settles and dressers were originally made for the farmhouses and cottages. The expansion of overseas trade in the eighteenth century included imports as well as exports, and amongst the former were fine woods such as mahogany, which became fashionable for the lighter, more elegant furniture of the period. Consequently many old pieces discarded by the gentry found their way into farmhouses and cottages whose furnishings naturally lagged behind those of their richer and more important neighbours. Then, in their turn, the farmer's wives and daughters influenced by Victorian gentility and fashion replaced the old oak furniture by modern articles, unfortunately at a period when machine-made furniture was of poor design and lacking in craftsmanship. This was made easy by the travelling dealers in secondhand goods who offered ready cash or an exchange of new goods and bamboozled many an innocent woman out of treasures she did not know were valuable. And there were also occasions in the farming slumps of the 1930s when butter and eggs fetched starveling prices and a farmer's wife was hard set to find money for necessities, when a five pound note was more important than an old carved chest or dresser.

Today the farm kitchen has changed completely. Composition tiles on the floor have taken the place of the old stone flags which took so long to scrub each week. A modern sink unit instead of the old hand pump over a yellow pot trough, crockery stowed away behind the sliding glass doors of wall cupboards instead of the open shelves, a slow combustion stove in gleaming white enamel instead of the monstrous black range or crane and spit; no working woman could possibly feel nostalgia for the old kitchens, though they were cosy enough on a winter evening

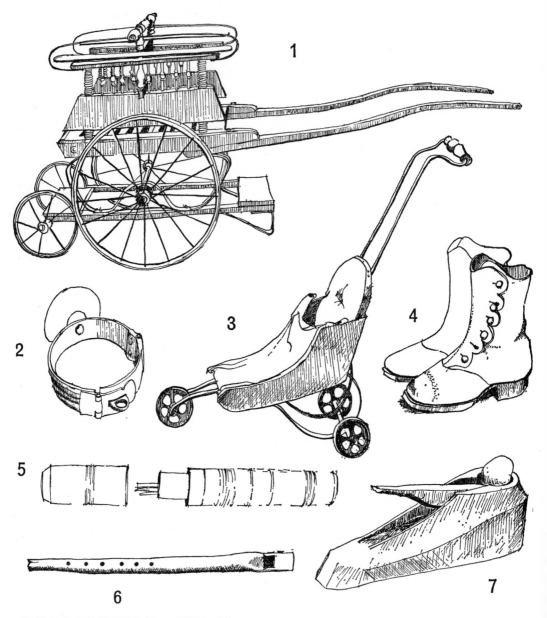

CHILDREN'S TOYS. *From Filkins Museum*

*1: Victorian mailcart for two children. 2, Armlet used to hold truant child to wall or desk; late nineteenth century. 3, Toy pram; price 1s. 6d. in 1900. 4, Child's button boots. 5, George Swinford's slate box. 6, George Swinford's tin whistle. 7, Tip-ball game.*

with the settle in place, the curtains closed and a bright fire with the pig swill in its iron pot bubbling merrily or a kettle on the hob.

The revival in the making of good furniture came about because the mass-produced things appalled such men as William Morris and his disciples by their tastelessness and the abandonment of the principles of good craftsmanship. And if the result of Morris's teaching was not the revival of good furniture in the cottages and homes of the working class in town or countryside, it did keep the old crafts from dying out and gave them recognition amongst the few. For ordinary people the handmade article was too expensive; in most instances they preferred the factory-made as being more up to date, for the young have always wanted to be released from the old things and the old ways.

The Cotswolds at that time were a little-known part of England, a rural district cut off by the narrow hill roads from quick communication with London and the big centres of industry, exporting a little agricultural produce to local markets and with its own unemployment problems. It still lived more in the past than in the future, with only a small part of its cloth trade kept alive at Stroud, where steam-power had been installed in the mills, the other mills closed or turned over to concerns hoping to make money in an area of cheap labour but often defeated after a few years by poor transport and lack of capital. Morris, sickened by the get-rich-quick attitude that was making areas of England hideous with its factories and streets of mean dwellings under the grime and shadow of factory chimneys, saw in the Cotswolds an unspoiled countryside and a place where the old way of life still perisisted, where the blacksmiths, the carpenters and joiners, the masons and wheelwrights went on in the same old way as they had done for centuries.

This discovery of the Cotswold craftsman and the Cotswold style of building affected a wide circle of artists, craftsmen and writers associated with Morris, particularly in his Society for the protection of Ancient Buildings, and these people in turn set out to explore for themselves this delectable land. C. R. Ashbee established a Guild of Craftsmen in 1902, and moved to Chipping Campden with his men, hoping their influence would bring back some of the old skills and make it possible to earn a living by these skills; and though this was a hope that failed because of the harsh economics of the period, the Guild had a lasting effect on the little town and helped to a better understanding of good work.

The chief people in this modest revolution were Ernest Gimson, an architect, the Barnsley brothers and Norman Jewson. Their aim was not to perpetuate the past but to use its skills and knowledge to enrich the present and future. Gimson's creed was directly inspired by Morris, that is the deep satisfaction of making useful and beautiful things, and he believed that a natural art could only come about by keeping alive the old traditions and developing them. He left London and with the brothers Ernest and Sidney Barnsley of Birmingham set up workshops at Sapperton on the borders of Cirencester Park, a small village in a secluded wooded valley, encircled by hills and reached at that time by steep and winding packhorse trails. Here for twenty-six years he lived and worked, and the working companionship of the older workmen of the area who had been brought up in the traditions and skills of their forefathers were his constant inspiration.

The most important mansion in the Cotswold vernacular style, Rodmarton Manor (Pl. 8), was built between 1909 and 1926 by Ernest Barnsley. Rodmarton Manor could be seen as the culmination of that style, a final and perfect flowering in every particular; one cannot imagine that circumstances, architect, craftsmen, the desire and the means will ever come together again. Ernest and Sidney Barnsley were originally furniture makers, but after he settled in Sapperton Ernest worked mainly as architect and builder. He made his own drawings and closely supervised every detail of the structure and fittings down to the smallest item, using stone from the estate quarries and timber from its woods sawn on the pit and seasoned in traditional fashion.

Alfred Bucknell, the son of a Sapperton wheelwright, was responsible for most of the ironwork. He had learned the elements of the craft of blacksmith from his father but it was Gimson who recognized his potential genius and, taking him as an apprentice, taught him to make strap hinges, latches and casements, wrought-iron gates and grilles and to work also in copper, brass and steel. Some of Bucknell's finest work is to be seen in Rodmarton Manor together with that of F. Baldwin, another craftsman in metal. Many others of that band of craftsmen who lived and worked at Sapperton contributed their best work, including Peter Waals, H. Davol, both cabinet makers, who also interpreted some of Gimson's finest designs (Pls 68, 71, 73, 74). The majority of the pieces from the Sapperton workshops were much too expensive for ordinary use and have now become museum pieces, but the spirit which inspired them came from the Cotswold tradition of craftsmanship and there are still old men in the neighbourhood who were trained in the Sapperton workshops and who remember the high quality of workmanship and try to pass it on to the younger generation.

One traditional piece of furniture continued to be made for many years on Cotswold by one of the men trained by Gimson. This is the rushbottom chair which Gimson first made using a pole-lathe, an example of his keen interest in the earlier tools of the woodworker. Gimson had found an old man, Philip Clissett in Bosbury, Herefordshire, who made chairs by turning the parts on a pole-lathe and seating them with rushes he prepared himself, and Gimson learnt the craft from him (Pl. 70). With the permission of Mr Gardiner, who worked a saw mill at Sapperton, he put up his lathe in the mill, using its water-power. As the saw mill was not busy at that time Mr Gardiner's son, Edward, was given the job of assistant, and he proved so good at the job that Gimson turned the chair-making over to him, the agreement being that he designed the chairs and Edward Gardiner made them and they shared the profits. This was the beginning of a successful partnership. In 1913 Edward Gardiner moved to Leamington to extend the business, but the First World War interrupted his progress. After the war, in 1919 Sidney Barnsley asked him to make sixty chairs for the memorial library at Bedales School, which Gimson had designed just before he died. From that order came many others, including one from the Dean and Chapter of Coventry Cathedral. Finally Edward Gardiner moved to Priors Marston near Rugby to continue chair-making as a full-time occupation, using electric motor-power and a thermostatically controlled drying house for the timber, in fact combining new and old in a fashion which would have won the approval not only of Gimson but of the grand old master, William Morris himself.

Gimson was buried in Sapperton Churchyard under one of the ancient yews flanking the pathway to the church, his memorial a plain flat stone tomb with E. W. Gimson, 1919 engraved on a small bronze plate in the style characteristic of the district from the seventeenth century onwards. On the opposite side of the path beneath another great yew tree are the tombstones of the Barnsley brothers who were his friends and fellow craftsmen.

# The Dairy

THE dairy in the old days was one of the pleasantest places on the farm. Cool, clean and quiet, the slate or stone shelves, the white flagged floor, the shining pails and large flat dishes, the louvred or netted windows, the whitewashed walls and the lack of the usual litter of the other outhouses gave it a charm all its own. One perceptive child I knew once referred to a neighbour's dairy, where we used to go to buy butter and large jugs of buttermilk, as a temple, and when I asked her why she replied: 'It must be. Otherwise why do people whisper in there instead of shouting as they do outside?' Afterwards I took special notice of this and was amused to find that I, as well as Mrs Mitchell, the farmer's wife, spoke quietly there, while her somewhat rumbustious husband, who always began shouting for whatever he wanted when at least a hundred yards away, also dropped his voice a little when he appeared at the dairy door, though this may have been because he was obliged to take off his mucky rubber boots before he set foot on the snowy flags, for though he was master in his own house and tramped through it in boots dripping mud and manure he was afraid of the consequences if he did the same in the dairy. It was the one place where he acknowledged that his wife ruled.

It has always been a woman's province and from medieval times and possibly earlier until the beginning of the twentieth century the womenfolk of the smaller gentry—and of some of the greater—and the wives of large farmers never considered dairywork beneath them. They might have dairymaids for the actual work but they supervised the making of the butter and cheese. The novels of Jane Austen, George Eliot and others make it very plain that it was the job of the mistress to look after the dairy.

In the small dairy where there was no separator and in the days before separators were used the cream was skimmed off with a hand-skim, a saucer-shaped ladle with small holes which allowed the milk to drain through. The milk is first put to stand in large flat pans, which on Cotswold were usually made of crockery with glaze only on the inside, made by the nearest pottery, often small village concerns who

DOMESTIC BYGONES. *From Filkins Museum*

*1. Cooking spatula. 2, Cooking tongs. 3, 'Salamander', heated iron for browning griddle cakes. 4, Baker's wooden dough trough. 5, Corer made of bone. 6, Milk dipper. 7, Milk pail. 8, Farmworker's 'frail'.*

catered for local needs. In the Filkins Museum, for instance, there are pans over a hundred years old made by a firm at Charlbury, and it is only in recent years that the pottery was closed. Such firms made bowls for bread-making and other domestic uses, and during the late nineteenth century when tin vessels became available they went over to making flowerpots as farmers' wives began to imitate the gentry in having a conservatory for flowering plants to adorn their drawing rooms.

The unglazed exterior of these pans helped to keep the milk cool and sweet, very necessary in the days before refrigerators. Skimming the cream from a pan of milk is a pleasant job, one gets a kind of sensuous enjoyment as one puts the skimmer under the thick crust of cream and it crinkles in smooth heavy ripples. After skimming, the cream is put into another bowl and left until churning day.

Although every dairymaid knows that butter will finally 'come', there is always a little anxiety about the churning. There are traditional tales about butter that refused to 'come' however long the churning. One of the common misdeeds of witches was putting a spell on the dairy so that however long the churn was turned that steady splish splash would never change to the dull thud, thud, of the butter going round in the buttermilk. Mrs Mitchell said it was a job you could not hurry, when it wanted to come it would in its own time, as if the butter had a will of its own, and if you started churning hoping to be finished at a certain time then you could be sure it would defeat you. Modern machinery has eliminated the risks and fantasies from modern butter-making, yet one wonders is it sentimentality that makes butter made in an old-fashioned churn, washed and patted into shaped and then impressed as a final flourish with a pattern of rose or cow, taste so much better than the factory product?

Once the butter had formed, the remaining part of the process was straightforward; that is, the hobgoblin element was no longer able to play tricks. There was the washing in the churn after the buttermilk had been drained away through the bunghole at the bottom and the cold water poured in and the butter swished round it in; and then, pale and glistening, the butter was taken out. After this all possible water was worked out and salt added, the two processes going together. When this was done—and if all possible water was not taken out the butter would not keep—it was shaped into rounds, or slabs, the pounds and the half-pounds. Unless the butter was being made for market, weighing was not necessary, and when it was, an experienced dairymaid was able to guess the weight without scales.

Farm butter, except when cream from Channel Island cows is used, is paler than butter made in factories, where colouring matter is added, it having been found that a yellow colour suggests greater richness, just as brown eggs are more popular than white though the colour of eggshell or butter has nothing to do with taste or goodness. A method sometimes used by dairymaids to colour butter, particularly autumn butter, was to use marigold flowers. These were put in an earthenware pot and covered with a layer of salt, layers of flowers and salt being added until the pot was filled. Then it was covered to keep it airtight, being closely covered again each time a few flowers were taken out. These were pounded with a pestle in a wooden bowl, the juice strained after being mixed with a little skim milk and then squeezed through muslin into the cream before it was put into the churn.

New scientific methods of butter-making spread very slowly, but in the last quarter of the nineteenth century the offering of prizes for butter at the Royal Agricultural Society's shows, and at the county and smaller shows, and the printing of articles in journals and local papers about the new methods, led to a great improvement in the quality and to the elimination of 'witchcraft' theories and the erratic behaviour of the cream in the churn. The Cotswolds, however, did not sell butter in a big way; this was left to the lowland farms of Gloucestershire, with their rich meadows and large dairy herds. On the hill farms the farmer's wife and the dairymaids continued in the old fashion for the most part until the factories took over and butter-making for sale by the farmer's wife was no longer economic.

## DOUBLE GLOUCESTER CHEESE

Butter was never exported in large quantities from the Cotswolds but its cheese was famous. Large quantities were made on the dairy farms in the Vale of Berkeley and Severn but Cotswold farms also supplied a good portion for export to the big cities and overseas. Double Gloucester's special quality depended on the right ripening and even more on the correct kind of feed for the cows whose milk provided the raw material for cheese-making. If the herbage was too rich, then the cheese tended to 'heave', so that the lush water-meadows of the valleys were not as suitable as the grassy hillsides with their thinner grasses and variety of small herbs. Countrymen today are stubborn in their belief that the cheese made on the farm when they were young, before the cattle were fed on silage or temporary leys but existed chiefly on the short sweet turf and hay of the wolds, was far superior to the cheese made today.

The making of Double Gloucester was county-wide and spilled over into Oxfordshire, Warwickshire and Worcestershire. Cheese made by Mrs Jeffries at Briar Hill Farm, Broad Campden, and ripened in the attic was being sold at Banbury in 1880. Banbury was known for its Cheese Fairs, and at Ebrington, a few miles away, up to the Second World War a unique Cow Charity distributed surplus milk which was made into cheese and shared amongst the villagers. This was made after the manner of Double Gloucester but on cottage scale; the large round shallow dishes for the milk, the simple press, the special cheese-cloths, the ripening period in loft or attic away from the light—and then the pleasure of eating it. This was a Charity which brought more prayers for the founder's soul, more appreciation of his benevolence than that of the usual doles of bread or pence. 'It was summut good to fill our bellies when there was more dinner times than dinners', as one old man put it. With a hunk of Cow Charity cheese, a slice of bread made from wheat grown on the allotment and ground at Pudlicot Mill and a jug of cider to wash it down 'you knew you'd summut unside you'.

Cheese-making was one of those jobs on the farm that women did better than men (Pl. 81). It was not arduous but it could not be forgotten, for there was something to be done to it every day and the mistiming of any part of the process could ruin the cheese. Even when it was made and put to ripen in the cheese room or attic the cheeses had to be turned and looked at at intervals, the temperature of the room noted, the windows opened and shut accordingly; in fact, as one women told me, 'you had to like the job and keep it in mind all the time'.

Farmhouses had their own cheese-rooms (Pls 82, 84–5). They can be recognized today by their louvred windows and the racks where the cheeses were laid to ripen and, if there has been no clean sweep of old utensils, by an old cheese-press of stone or iron, wooden cheese vats usually made by a local cooper of oak with lids of elm, and very rarely the cheese 'kettle'. The earlier ones of copper or brass, an expensive item of equipment, have mostly disappeared from the farm but can occasionally be found in an antique shop or, the pride of a flower-arranger, holding tasteful arrangements of flowers and plants in a drawing-room. The later kettles were made of tin and some were good examples of the tinsmith's craft, but when discarded and neglected they soon rusted away into holes.

One farmer's wife I knew always hung her cheese-cloths to dry on a ragged bush of southernwood growing by the cheese-room door, another would not have the wormwood and elder growing on the triangle of waste ground near the dairy cut down, because she said it kept the flies away. She took her cheese and butter once a week to market, where she had her special customers, making her stall attractive with snowy cheese-cloth covering her wares as well as her stall, with butter wrapped in clean rhubarb leaves. Her customers were willing to pay the few extra pence for these niceties. A good saleswoman as well as a good dairywoman, she would discuss cheese with her customers, who were mostly men buying cheese and women buying butter. The men liked to taste the cheese and she encouraged this, flattering their taste, I suspect, so they bought her wares.

It was from her I learned that 'hay' cheese made in the winter months when the cattle were kept in the yard, was a hard cheese, while summer or 'grass' cheese made from the milk of cows fed on the first sweet bite of early summer was the best of all, suitable for children and invalids as well as adults.

Some farms were noted locally for their cheese although it was not always these who won the prizes at shows, for the working farmers' wives and daughters seldom had time for the finishing touches necessary to catch the judge's eye. Cheese-tasting had its own rituals as solemn as those for tasting wine or tea, for in the days when it was difficult to control temperature and humidity in the cheese-rooms unforeseen things could happen not apparent until the tester had thrust his implement into the centre and, after a keen look and a keen sniff at the withdrawn morsel (for eyes and nose as well as taste-buds came into the business), found conclusive evidence as it went into his mouth.

The price for farmhouse cheese slumped so badly in the 1930s that it was no longer possible to continue making it on the farm. The cheese-makers had seen the slow decline but kept hoping with each season that the price would rise. When it dropped to sixpence a pound and less at Stow, Banbury, Cirencester and other markets the farmers' wives and daughters, although accustomed to working for very little return, realized it was the end. The farms geared to cheese-making, where the cows calved in March and cheese was made from the milk of cows grazed on summer pastures from May to early autumn, either sold their milk in bulk or turned over to butter-making, though the price of butter also was declining. Wages were low and there was much unemployment, and colonial cheese was cheap, so one more good local food ceased to be produced; when the factories finally took over, the making of cheese on the farm became a luxury product for home consumption and a few connoisseurs willing to pay for it.

A large number of machines were invented in the nineteenth century for use in butter- and cheese-making but on the whole this did not affect the smaller farms and these were the main source of supply, with the work being done by family labour. Except in a few large dairy farms belonging to landowners interested in new methods, factories took over cheese-making with little transition from the earliest methods to the most modern. Seventeenth-century writers such as Robert Surflet were insistent that the farmer's wife must ensure the dairy was kept 'void of sowerness or sluttishness that a Prince's bedchamber must not exceed it', adding that 'none of her maides have anything to do with butter or cheese when they have their termes', which takes us back far into the taboos of the past. The utensils were buckets, milk pans, churns, cheese vats, straining cloths, a syle or soiling dish, a wooden bowl with the bottom cut out covered with a clean linen cloth that did not allow 'the least mote or hair to pass through it' with, of course, the hand of the dairymaid being the most important. We find mentions of cheese-presses in wills and inventories as early as 1620.

In 1663 at Broadway a dairymaid was paid £2 a year, and the long hours worked, often from four in the morning until ten at night, were considered normal, Arthur Young in 1804 actually recommended them. But soon after that time, in 1843, these long hours became a source of concern according to the report of the Law Commissioners on Employment of Women and Children in Agriculture of that date.

The difference between Single and Double Gloucester cheese was the thickness, Single being about two or three inches thick and weighing about fifteen pounds and Double four to five inches thick and weighing about twenty-four pounds. Both were approximately sixteen inches in diameter and were of similar quality, though some believe that the Single Gloucester ripened more speedily and had the best flavour.

Cheese from the Vale of Gloucester and the south Cotswolds was sent to Bath and Bristol, and from Bristol a considerable quantity was exported to the West Indies. Cheese for London went via Lechlade and the Thames. There were three sales a year, in July, Michaelmas and Spring, attended by factors who, knowing the dairies, took all the cheese they made often without first inquiring about price. Both Defoe and William Marshall praise Gloucestershire cheese, well established by the mid eighteenth century, though G. E. Fussell says there is no reference to it earlier than 1704, when it was extolled by Robert Morden in his *New Description and State of England*.

The usual method of making was to set the evening milk for cream and it was then skimmed. A part of the skimmed milk was heated and the whole added to the next morning's milk. If the milk was very rich, cream was sometimes taken from the morning milk as well. The curd was broken into pieces as big as peas and hot water or whey or a mixture of both poured on to it and the curd crumbled into the vat, then squeezed by hand and the vat tilted to let the whey run off. After repeating this process the curd, still in its cloth, was replaced in the vat and tucked in, the vat was then put in the press and pressed for about three hours, turned and pressed again till evening, when it was taken out and salt was rubbed into it. It was then pressed again, turned morning and evening for a couple of days, taken out and put on the rack. Pressing time was about twenty-four hours. For the next ten days the cheeses were turned at intervals, and it was by the duration and regularity of these intervals that a good cheese-maker showed her experience. After this period of turning the cheeses were soaked in whey for a few hours and then scraped smooth until the cheese looked neat and polished. A final rinsing in whey, a wipe with a cloth to get rid of the moisture, and the cheeses were then put on shelves to store and await buyers.

External painting to give a uniform finish, as well as the use of anatto (vegetable dye) for colouring the inside, were deplored by William Marshall but these practices became general and were expected on cheeses for export, though for local consumption they were not so usual.

# Cider, Plum Jerkum

CIDER (Pls 86–96) was the chief drink of the farmers and their men and was made in tremendous quantities. Norman Jewson wrote of 2,000 gallons being made by Gimson and the Barnsley brothers from one year's crop of apples and sold to local farmers around Sapperton. Mrs Wilks, a farmer's daughter, told me that when she was a child it was her job each morning to fill the wooden cider barrels and stone jars carried by the men into the fields. The foremen had gallon jars, the others half a gallon. This was their official allowance but if they needed more they could always come to the cider house for a refill. There was hospitality for all and whoever came to the farm, people delivering goods or messages, travellers, friends, all were invited to partake as a matter of course. The cider was kept in a special house, the great barrels raised on trestles so that it was easy to pour into jugs or other containers waiting there. She remembers the coolness of the cider house, her impatience at the time it took to fill the men's containers each morning, for the taps on the barrels were small.

Fruit grown on the light soil of the hills came smaller but was more agreeable to the taste. Most farms had their own cider orchards whose trees were rarely pruned but allowed to grow naturally. The best cider was made from a variety of apples, each giving its own quality to the cider, and the man who planted an orchard put in a mixture of trees.

Some villages were famous throughout the district for their cider. Taynton, on the Oxfordshire-Gloucestershire border near Burford, was known for producing, according to Rudder, 'a very rich and pleasant cider . . . and for an excellent kind of perry, made of the fruit called the Tainton Squash-pear'. William Marshall also notes 'the superior excellence of this squash-pear'. Rudge said 'it requires nice management, but if the process of fermentation be rightly conducted, it may well be called the champagne of England'. John Holder, who lived at Taynton at the beginning of the eighteenth century, noted in his diary in 1700, 'I bought and sett upp a Cyder Mill and presses att my dwelling house'. And in 1703 when tempests had ravaged the land, two hundred of his fruit trees were blown down. In 1713 he

86–87. *Cider mill (above) and cider press at Grove Court, Upton St Leonards, in use until the 1960s.*

88–91. *Cider making at Gastrell's Farm, Upton St Leonards. Left above, sacks of cider apples awaiting processing. Below, 'Joker' turning the mill to crush the fruit. Right, making up the pulp into a 'cheese' for pressing.*

92. *The tun-pail has a hole in its base aligned with the hole in the tun. The extracted juice is left to ferment in tun.*

93 & 94. *Cider bucket and tun-pail from Priory Farm, Leonard Stanley. The latter has not yet been made in plastic.*

95. *Cider cask at Woodford Green Farm, Berkeley;
7 foot high, with a capacity of 1,200 gallons.*

96. *Tap for an 8,000-gallon cider vat, with a standard
tap for comparison.*

97. *Cooper's marks on a stave of a cider barrel.*

98. *Farm waggon at harvest, Ebrington, about 1900.*

99. *Waggon built for his own use by J. Lock, carpenter and timber merchant of Cirencester. Discovered in the farmyard of Lower Field Farm, Ampney St Mary, it was restored for carnival use by Mr A. Hitchman of Poulton and Mr D. Penfold; it had previously been restored in 1912. Photographed at Ready Token.*

100. *Nameboard on a waggon at Randwick, with spelling based on the local pronunciation of 'Gloucestershire'.*

101 & 102. *Farm waggons at Humphreys End Farm, Randwick.*

103. *Waggon made by W. Major of Coaley, principal builder of the Stroud district; Little Britain Farm, Woodchester.*

104. *Farm trolley, Humphreys End Farm, Randwick.*

105. *Tip-cart, Little Britain Farm.*

106. *Tip-cart, Humphreys End Farm.*

*107. Goat cart; Ebrington, 1912.*

*108. Governess cart still in use, Quenington.*

109. *A series of wheelwrights' planes used by three generations of the Spicer family at Eastleach. In the collection of Mr R. Soule, Southrop.*

110. *Wheelwright's workshop, Paxford.*

111. *Hand-made waggon-shoe from Barnsley.*

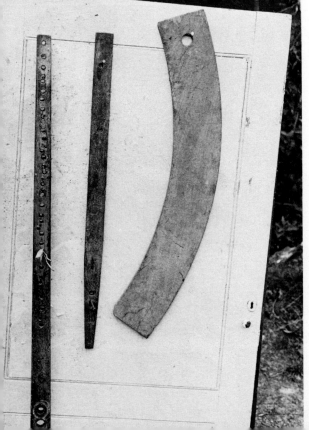

112. *Wheelwright's measures from Keytes of Paxford.*

113. *Anvil from old forge, Paxford.*

114. *'Swaging block' for shaping metal rods, etc.*

115. *Wheelwright's 'sweep'*
*for measuring different radii.*
*Mr Fred Saunders.*

116. *'Traveller' for measuring*
*the circumference of wheel and*
*tyre. Mr Fred Saunders.*

117. *Tool for making holes in*
*hubs. Collection of Mr R.*
*Soule.*

118. *Tyring-dogs for forcing red-hot tyres onto wheels. Mr Fred Saunders.*

119. *Wheel-bed, Paxford.*

120, 121. *Wheel and hub of waggons at Humphreys End Farm, Randwick.*
*A section of the hub could be removed for lubrication.*

122. *Rear hub of the waggon shown in Plate 99;*
*the 'eye' is for attaching additional traction.*

123. *Typical narrow Cotswold cartwheel. Manor*
*Farm, Southrop.*

'grafted the perry stocks with Huffcap', and the following year the cider stocks 'with Woodcocke'. 'I graft five rowes of stocks with twenty-one sorts of the most beautifull Red Apples I could procure (Woodcock and Redstreake excepted)', he wrote in 1725.

A vast tonnage of apples was bought from the lowlands of Gloucestershire, from Worcestershire, Herefordshire and Shropshire in years when late frosts nipped the Cotswold cider orchards. There was no finesse in the gathering. The trees were shaken, stripped, beaten, the fallers scooped up into baskets or 'kipes' and then tipped into a cart. Occasionally selected apples would be kept apart for a special brew but mostly all went into the great heaps left to sweat and mellow before being taken to the mill. The smell of decaying apples saturated the countryside for miles around. One woman told me the smell alone could make her feel drunk 'but then I never had no head for drink'. She liked cider best when it was new and called 'apple wine'; 'When we were kids we were allowed to have new cider—Mother said it opened the bowels and our teacher used to say she always knew when cider was being made because the kids were always putting up their hands to be excused. Mind you we did that to get out for a few minutes, going across the yard to the privies made a break, though they did stink.'

Not all cider was made by the farmer. Travelling cider-makers used to go from farm to farm, sometimes men who went on to cider-making after they had finished harvesting in gangs. The farmer supplied the press and the accessories, the apples, the horse if it was a horse-mill, the men the know-how and the labour. Crude as the process seems to an outsider it had to be understood, and as the same men, or the same leader of the gang, turned up year after year last year's brew would be talked over, its flavour assessed, praised, criticized. A great deal of the easy working of the farm for the following year depended on the cider, the farmworker regarding it as his right in the old days, part of his wages, in fact, and a good brew put heart into a man and gave that extra impetus to his limbs. When at the beginning of this century bottles of cold tea took the place of the little barrels of cider for drink in the fields, kept cool under a wall beside the frail containing his bread and cheese or hunk of fat bacon, the exchange was a poor one nutritiously. A draught of cider helped the digestion and generated a kind of contentment in a way a bottle of cold tea could never do even if it 'very nigh took the skin off your throat it was that sharp'.

It was never a woman's drink, until manufacturers produced a refined form in bottles. Having once been persuaded to try a glass of rough cider straight from the cask I can say with feeling that it is a drink for a strong head and a throat of iron, for its potency made my head swim while its harshness brought tears to my eyes and left the inside of my mouth feeling it had been sandpapered.

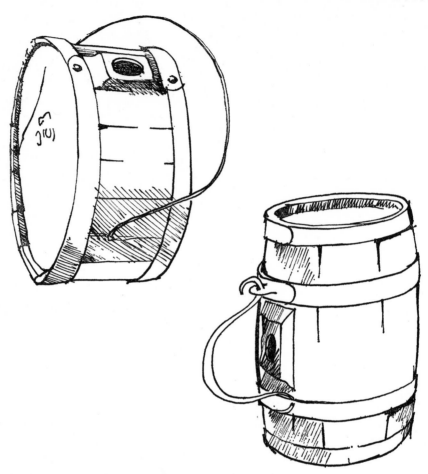

*Farmworkers' cider barrels; from Town Farm, Ebrington.*

The apparatus for making cider is simple enough, and consists of a circular stone trough or cistern; the runner or bruising stone; an upright axle-tree; cog wheel; a stirrer; reever and shovel. The trough, about 9 inches deep and 30 feet in circumference, is in three or four parts clamped together by a wheelwright. The bruising stone, about $3\frac{1}{2}$ feet in diameter, is flat on one side and slightly convex on the other and has a strong axle of wood fastened through it. The reever is a piece of board fixed to a wooden handle made to fit the trough and with this implement the pulp is drawn together and then carried to the press with a wooden shovel or scoop.

A smaller type operated by hand consists of two wooden cylinders toothed or indented, each about 9 inches in diameter enclosed in the way of other mills with a feeder at the top. The cylinders can be moved to a greater or lesser distance apart and are used first to cut the fruit and then brought closer together so that scarcely a kernel can pass unbroken. The grinding and breaking of the fruit to a fine pulp is of great importance, for much of the flavour of the cider comes from the kernels. The pulp is then carried to the press or laid up in tubs for twenty-four hours, which is said to make the best cider. The two upright pieces of oak kept in place by being let into the ground are called 'cheeks' or 'sisters'. The hair cloth is specially manufactured for the process, and the casks are fumigated before the racked liquor is poured into them. The old way of doing this, according to Rudge, was by using pieces of linen dipped in brimstone, set on fire and suspended in the casks for as long as they would burn. A later method was to take off the head of the cask and scrub the interior with hot water.

It was a common practice to put hunks of raw beef into the casks, which had completely disappeared by the time the casks were empty. One hears fearsome stories of the way in which in the old days farmers fortified their cider with dead rats or other animals but these, I imagine, are tales told in the pub when cider mugs have been filled and emptied many times and are meant to amaze and not to be taken literally. Apple maggots in plenty must have been in the pulp for there was little sorting out in the first stages, but fermentation would reduce extraneous matter to harmlessness and as the men who made the cider also drank it, even if their rule of thumb methods seem haphazard yet they had an understanding of the process without being able to explain it in scientific terms.

PLUM JERKUM

In the villages around Chipping Campden a favourite home-made wine was known as Plum Jerkum, once made by the farmers in huge quantities; today it is mostly the cottagers who make this heady brew. Plum orchards are to be found there, though many of these are fast disappearing, the trees bearing a dark damson-like fruit not unlike a bullace, and it is from this fruit the best plum jerkum is made. The men are responsible for plum jerkum, the women preferring to make cowslip, dandelion and elderberry, but on the whole it was and still is the men who make the home-made wines, leaving the more refined cordials, cowslip and elderflower, to the women. As it is the men who consume the plum jerkum its seems only proper that they should make it. I have been given several recipes but though they follow the usual processes of home-made wine the recipes differ a little with each person and in most cases I do not think I have been given the complete recipes, for each maker hints at secret ingredients he prefers to keep to himself, which give it a special flavour or potency. Potent it certainly is if one believes only a small part of the stories told about it. The first glass seems so innocuous that the drinker is easily persuaded to have a refill, and then the trouble begins. Its colour ranges from a deep purple to a claret red, its flavour from a sticky sweetness to a sparkling tartness according to the variety of plums used and the years it has been kept. One bottle saved from a brew put down when the first child was born to a farmer friend and kept for the son's twenty-first birthday celebrations proved to be disappointing, the colour faded and the taste thin and sour. The farmer's wife finally used it as vinegar.

The making of cider, perry and other fermented drinks goes back into prehistory but Holinshed, writing of Winchcombe Abbey, says that the best wine there was called 'Theologicum, because it was had from the cleargie and religious men unto whose houses manie of the laitie would often send for bottles filled with the same being sure that they had neither drinke or be served of the worst or such as was mingled or brewed by the vintner', which goes to confirm the opinion in Chaucerian times that the monks understood good liquor. There is some evidence that wine from grapes grown on the slopes of the hills above Winchcombe and Hailes was made by the monks who served the abbeys.

Coopers' marks can be found on old barrels (Pl. 97). The staves were numbered after the barrel had been completed, the cooper getting inside for the purpose before fitting the top. Sometimes the staves were used again and show more than one number. Specially grown reeds were used between the staves to make the barrel water-tight, the cider causing the dried reed to 'plim'. Delivery men carried supplies of reeds in case barrels sprang a leak during transit.

# The Wheelwright

'THE Gloucestershire waggon is beyond argument the best farm waggon I have seen in the kingdom. I know not a district which might not profit by its introduction,' wrote William Marshall in his *Rural Economy of Gloucestershire*, published in 1789. He might also have added that the reason for its shapeliness arose out of the kind of ground it was required to traverse, the loads it was built to carry, with that extra touch of grace Cotswold craftsmen in the old days could not resist adding to their work.

English farm waggons can be classified roughly into two types, the box waggon made for the lowlands, and the bow waggon for hill country, and these two kinds were well established by the end of the eighteenth century, having evolved from the rectangular box on wheels one sees pictured on illuminated manuscripts and the medieval baggage waggon. With tyres and wheels improving through the centuries, it had ambled its way from village to market town and back again until the 1900s. It is interesting that those early carriers' waggons were spindle-sided, as were the Cotswold farm waggons.

Bow waggons have very wide sideboards curving over large, greatly-dished wheels, the shallow waisted body and the arching sideboards giving a light and elegant appearance to the whole vehicle. Despite the shallow body, the carrying capacity is considerable because of the overhanging sideboards. A Cotswold-type waggon was a natural evolution from the early harvest cart or wain, that is, the English form of the continental ox-cart, and until a few years ago there were still people who remembered seeing them pulled by a team of oxen.

Tusser's '*Horse, oxen, cart, wagon or wain*
*The Lighter and Stronger, the greater they gain*',
made good sense on Cotswold where the many steep hills made it necessary for a waggon to be as lightweight as possible. This was achieved by the shallow body and by shaving away all superfluous wood from those parts of the frame not liable to strain. The various chamfers were picked out in red and black, adding to its pleasing appearance.

The Cotswold version of the bow waggon had its large wheels narrow to make movement easier on hilly ground, and the shallow body consisted of many iron or wooden spindles joining the inner top-rail to the frame (Pl. 102). The inner and outer top rails were crooked, bending arch-wise over the rear wheels and rising back and front, the ends of the outer top-rails projecting backwards beyond the line of the body. The forward side frames were bent inward to the main crossbar, providing a deep waist for the turning of the fore wheels. It was these arched rails and the waisted body which gave the waggon its air of elegance. The wide sideboards were also made of wooden or iron spindles, of wood in the earliest waggons but in the later ones of iron. On Cotswold, plank-sided waggons never superseded traditional types and when waggons began to be manufactured on a large scale farmers who did not have them made by local firms insisted upon traditional patterns and colour. The western escarpment marks the limit of this type; in the Severn Valley panel-sided instead of spindled bow waggons were common.

The main colour was yellow for the body with venetian red for the under-carriage and the rave bands picked out in black; the inscription on the front board was in red and black on a yellow background, the board so shallow that the name of the farmer and his farm almost fills it. Freshly painted, a waggon must have been a gay sight, especially when filled with yellow sheaves of corn, or with children in their best clothes setting forth on a Sunday School Outing.

Local wheelwrights made their own paint, grinding the pigments with rounded stones known as mullers. The main constituent was white lead, with yellow ochre, venetian red and lamp black. Every few years the waggons went back to the work-shop for repainting, and I know of one old waggon left to rot in a field for the past fifteen years where the black curlicues around the lettering are still as richly black as when they were painted. The iron work has kept its covering of black paint and looks as good as new.

Ash was used for the top-rails because of its strength and flexibility. Don Keyte, wheelwright and carpenter of Paxford, told me his grandfather reserved ash poles for this purpose and until recently he still had a store left over from the 1900s when the last waggon was made in his workshop. The hubs or 'stocks' of the wheels were of elm, and after being cut and bored they were chained together and put into a stream to soak for a few months, and then left to dry and season; your true crafts-man made sure he had a supply of well-seasoned stocks not only for his own use but for the sons or grandsons who might come after him. Don Keyte showed me curved and cut timber left by his grandfather and father, seasoned for the next job.

The spokes were made of oak and these were not sawn but split along the natural line of cleavage so no hidden weakness was concealed. The felloes of the big wheels were always of elm, with ash for the smaller wheels. Later, when waggons were made by large firms and not to order for a particular farmer by a local wheelwright, hickory wood was used, but for the waggons made locally the timber was chosen by the wheelwright and in many instances actually felled by him and then laid aside to season. The shafts—'sharves'—were of ash, and in some instances curved to the horses used, but this was a refinement and not common practice. Elm boarding made the bed of the waggon, and I have noticed that it is always the bed boards which go first when a waggon is left to rot, perished by water lying on them and slowly rotting the timber.

The tongue pole, the long squared piece of timber forming part of the under-carriage running on the back carriage to the centre or main pin, that is the pivot on which the undercarriage swivels, is also made of ash, while the cross piece at the front of the undercarriage is of oak, in two pieces, one on the frame and one on the carriage with the centre pin passing through both.

The wheels were strake-tyred, the strakes or strips of iron placed into position through holes prepared for them; a gap was left between the strakes to allow for expansion. Double strakes were common on very wide wheels, but waggons for hill farms more usually had narrow wheels and single strakes. Bonding the solid hoop of iron that was the tyre tightened the felloes and spokes into their places.

What Marshall called its most striking peculiarity is 'of having a crooked side-rail bending archwise over the hind wheel. This lowers the general bed of the waggon without lessening the diameter of the wheels. . . .' High wheels were important in rutted fields and on farm roads crudely surfaced with stone, the holes filled in with loose rubble and on steep hillsides with ruts scored deep by storm water.

The waggon was equipped for braking with a roller scotch and drag-shoe, never with a dog stick, the roller scotch being a small cylinder hung on chains behind a wheel when moving uphill to be handy for scotching immediately so that the waggon would not run downhill if stopped suddenly; carters were very aware of this problem in a district where gradients are considerable. The cylinder was usually made of elm wood bound with two iron bands and about nine inches long and five inches in diameter. It hung on the back axle when not in use.

The drag-shoe or skid-pan was a shaped piece of cast iron hung by a chain just in front of one of the rear wheels (Pl. 111). When going downhill the shoe was slipped under the wheel so that the wheel skidded instead of rotating and the wear and tear was taken by the sole of the shoe and not the tyre. The skid pan was about a foot long and its width was calculated according to the width of the tyre.

In a field near my home an old waggon lies rotting in a bed of nettles, left there after carrying its last load of hay some twenty years ago. A carter who worked on the farm for many years until he retired described this waggon to me as the easiest and best he had ever known. During the twenty-odd years he looked after it, it had never been taken back for repairs, only to be repainted; in fact he could not remember its ever needing repairs though the ground it traversed was rough and

*The waggon made by Keyte's of Paxford in 1884.*

hillocky. It was not taken out every day, carts were used for the daily carriage of foodstuffs and other things about the farm and fields, but was kept mainly for haytime and harvest. In the evening before the carters finished for the day it was taken to the brook, brushed out and washed down and then put into the cart-shed until it was wanted again. All the carts had to be left clean and washed every evening except one in constant use. The farmers and the carters were proud of their waggons and on a well-run farm they were looked after. They may not have known Tusser's

> '*Let cart be well searched without and within*
> *Well clouted and greased ere hay time begin*'

but they followed his precept.

The family firm of Keyte's of Paxford made this waggon in 1884. A member of the family, Don Keyte, told me it probably took about three months to make and that it was his father's custom to sign his waggons by incorporating into the front board what they called the 'baby's bottom', a personal rendering of the pair of spectacles design which Jenkins says was introduced into England from Scotland when large numbers of waggons were exported into the eastern counties. Waggons were usually made during the winter months and the profit was small, but the waggons were returned every four years for repainting and for repairs and over-hauling and, of course, they would have any other business from the farm. It was also an advertisement for the firm's craftsmanship, for every waggon and cart carried their name as well as the name of the farmer. They were proud of their work, a reputation for good craftsmanship was as important to them as big profits.

The waggon now falling into decay in the field, a Gloucestershire type made for an Ebrington farmer, was the last produced in Mr Keyte's workshop, but the special tools, the templates for the spokes, the patterns for the felloes, even the old bench where the parts were painted can still be seen in the workshop (Pl. 110). This was not the narrow-wheeled waggon of the hills, much of the Ebrington land being heavy with a layer of clay over stone brash, and the wheels made wider because of it. In all other respects it was a typical Cotswold waggon. This was the way the old wheelwrights worked, they knew the farm and adapted their work accordingly, and they also knew the farmers and the farmers knew them. These personal relationships meant that little extra put into the job which no mass-produced product could achieve.

The measuring devices were made in the workshop, flat pieces of wood marked in notches, but they were accurate; there was no place for rule of thumb if a waggon was to run sweetly. The 'hearth' still remained, a rectangular framework of brick rather like a small table. The smith built up his hearth to the right height to save himself unnecessary strain in lifting as he transferred the iron from anvil to forge and back again for heating, and tempering. The bed of coke, 'smith's breeze', or small fuel known as 'beans', was laid in the centre. The fire-pit was about 3 or 4 feet square and consisted mostly of unburnt fuel ready to be raked into the fire as it was needed, the actual fire being only a few inches across. The fire had to be con-centrated, otherwise the heat would have been too intense for the smith to get near it.

A special shovel or slice with a long handle was used to scoop up the fuel to put on the fire, and a small rake or hook-like tool to remove clinkers, and these im-plements with his tongs hung on a rail about the hearth. A twiggy brush to sprinkle water on the fire when he wanted to reduce heat also stood nearby. Timing is the art of smith and wheelwright, together with deftness in handling heavy material. Strength must be tuned to muscular control, for there is delicate work to be done as well as the mighty pounding of the hammer.

A waggon formerly in the Gloucester Folk Museum but now in the Reading Museum of English Rural Life, must be one of the last waggons to be made on

Cotswold. It was built for W. Haines and Sons of Westington. Pulled by tractors instead of horses, waggons continued in use on farms as late as 1950, but hay-balers, combine harvesters, corn-drying equipment had by then taken over and the making of new waggons with their elaborate iron and timber work was no longer economic. Almost overnight, it seems, they had become museum pieces, memorials to the wheelwrights, blacksmiths and carpenters of another age.

# The Blacksmith

THE history of the smith on Cotswold is a fascinating one. The tribe of Dobuni who inhabited the district before the Roman occupation were skilled metal workers, as excavations at Bagendon revealed, and one has only to look at the variety and excellence of the iron tools and other metal objects found in the Cirencester area and exhibited in the Corinium Museum to realize that they went on exercising their craft long after they had left their ancient hill-top settlement to become citizens of Corinium, and in later years, Cirencester.

In those days pagan belief in the smith's magical powers set him apart from the rest of the tribe, and when in Christian times medieval churchmen invented stories of the smith defeating the devil by his own greater cunning and by crude humorous devices such as pulling Old Nick's nose with redhot tongs or making him sweat over the anvil it did not entirely dispel the aura of black magic. The paraphernalia of his trade encouraged it; the dusky forge when the fire roared to white-hot heat and the sparks flew, the hissing of the metal as it was plunged into water, these things could not but bring to mind pictures of hell-fire in the days when the torments of hell were as much part of religious teaching as the delights of heaven.

As the centuries went by the image of Vulcan the smith-god degenerated into a bogeyman to frighten little children. An old lady of my acquaintance told me her mother used to threaten her with the smith when she had tried her patience beyond endurance. But if the folk memory of his dark powers faded he still remained the most important of the village tradesmen until he disappeared from village life altogether. Carpenter, mason, baker, tailor, butcher, cobbler, at a pinch their work could be done by most handymen, but only a smith could shoe a horse, put an iron tyre on a cart wheel, make a harrow, or beat out a shepherd's crook.

A village smith needed a wide knowledge of the equipment of all the other trades, the metal parts of the bakehouse, hinges for the carpenter, iron clamps for the masons, and tools for them all: the heavy domestic articles, iron pots and spits, hearth cranes, grates, fire-dogs—the list is endless. The farmer could not do without him. Seed drills, binders, tow-bars, pitchforks, scythes are only a few of the

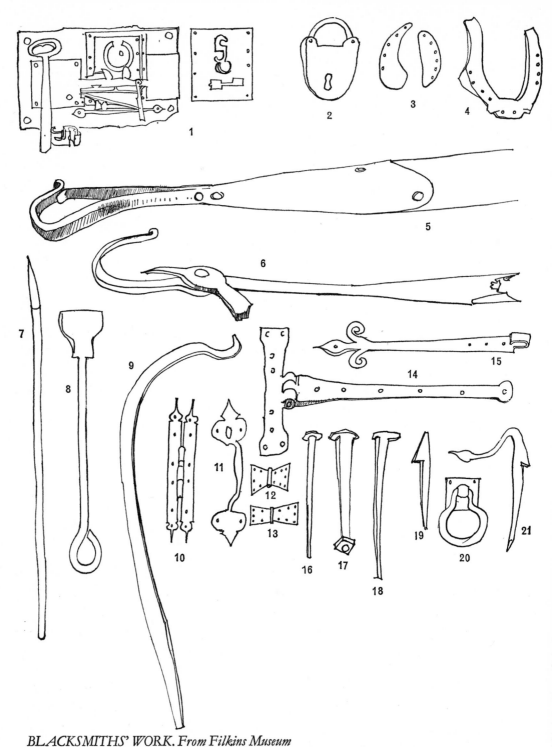

BLACKSMITHS' WORK. *From Filkins Museum*

*1. Lock and key. 2, Padlock. 3, Ox shoes ('cues'). 4, Horseshoe. 5,6, Well hooks. 7, Ox goad.*
*8, Lamb's tail cutter. 9, Hook to stick in ground for women to hang kettle or cooking pot on when*
*leasing. 10, 12–15, Hinges. 11, Door handle. 16–18, Bolts for coach. 19–21, Door fasteners.*

articles he was called upon to make or mend or sharpen, and he had also to forge the large nuts and bolts needed for the repairs. The tremendous number of iron items of all shapes and sizes in general use from the Middle Ages onward surprises a visitor visiting a Folk Museum, as well as the fine quality of the work. George Swinford's Museum at Filkins near Burford has a collection gathered over the years from local sources, and he can relate the history and give the name of the maker of each piece in most cases; and the Folk Museum at Gloucester has some fine examples of the work of wheelwrights and blacksmiths and their tools.

I once asked a smith how he knew the function of the myriad pieces of iron-ware he had to handle in his work. He said that farmers often preferred to go on using an old tool rather than obtain a new one if it had served its purpose well, and he had learned more by handling articles made in the old days when there were no standardized factory parts or implements than in any other way. Carrying this to its logical conclusion, the newest articles should show the result of this accumulated experience of ages, but this no longer applies to ordinary ware, only to those special handmade things which have become expensive luxuries; not what another old friend called 'common tackle'. It was the common tackle which made up the bulk of the village smith's work, and until the middle of the nineteenth century he was indispensable. He had a brief come-back during the last war when it was difficult for the farmer to get new machinery and it was essential to grow as much food as possible. Then every available smith was working to his limit to keep the old machines in order.

Each village had its smithy; larger ones often had two, one whose main work was shoeing horses, another for general work, and there were travelling smiths who went round the farms and riding stables shoeing horses. These travelling smiths operate today now most village smithies have closed down, for shoeing not working horses but those kept for riding. In every Cotswold town less than fifty years ago there were several smiths each specializing in different branches of the work. But it is the village smith who did a little of everything, from making an iron hook with a spike to stick into the ground for the women who went leasing (gleaning) with their children to hang their cooking pots on, to shoeing oxen and horses or mending a plough, who is remembered today when something needs repairing and no large firms are willing to do the job because it is too small for them to make a good profit.

One of the articles to be found in a smithy hanging on the walls amongst the iron chains was a shut-link, 'the carter's friend'. It was used for joining chains, especially those on harness, and consisted of two semi-circular pieces of iron made after the style of a split key ring, which when it was slid open turned into a spare link. Lengths of iron chains came from the foundry, the shut-links were often made by the blacksmith as one of the examples of his craft. As one said to me many years ago when I had taken a shut-link to him I had found in my garden, 'That's one of the most useful things on a farm. My old Dad taught me how to make them and a tricky job it was. I was proud when I'd made one to his satisfaction. My old Dad might have made the very one you found, or my grandad, for we've always been smiths as long back as I remember. I'm the last one and when I finish there's no-body to take over. I only keep going because of the racing stables.' And he pointed to the wall behind him where hung a row of used racehorse plates.

I escaped then because I had heard many times of the exploits of these particular animals and how he always kept the old shoes of the winners, and how much he won or lost on them. It was 1938 and his business was in a bad way except for this one job, which at least provided him with free drinks at the pub because of his association with the racing stables. He had been a man of magnificent physique, tall, broad, with a thick crop of black curly hair, such a man as might have inspired Longfellow, with his large and sinewy hands and the muscles of his brawny arms as strong as iron bands. It was said in the village he had fathered more illegitimate children than he had fingers on those same hands, which one could well believe for he still had a way with him though when I knew him he was sixty years old with thinning hair, a paunch and red-veined purplish cheeks. The decline of his trade and of his authority, because as his strength and trade declined so did his prestige in the village, the death of his wife who had never borne him a child, and the dissipation of his earlier years, all these things were slowly eating away his health and strength, though he could still swing a mighty hammer on occasion.

The smithy of Mr Soden at Idbury has been turned into a shop where the villagers sell their home-made bread, cakes, jams and surplus garden produce and it no longer holds the tools of his trade, but a massive stone trough made of a single piece of stone remains to remind one of the village mason as well as the smith.

The bellows have disappeared, but as in most Cotswold smithies they were likely to have been circular in a kind of wooden cradle, with five or six concertina-like leather folds. Bellows made their own music, a bubbling throaty sound, much pleasanter than the shrill whine of the electrically-driven fan used in modern smithies, but if the sound is not as pleasing the modern version of bellows gives more freedom to the smith. The handle of the oldfashioned bellows was a cowhorn, its curve turned downward, that being the direction required, a counterweight bringing the bellows up again and so producing a continuous draught.

The smith had his own names for the heats he required, homespun but expressive. Snowball for white heat, cherry red, blood red; full, light, slipper and

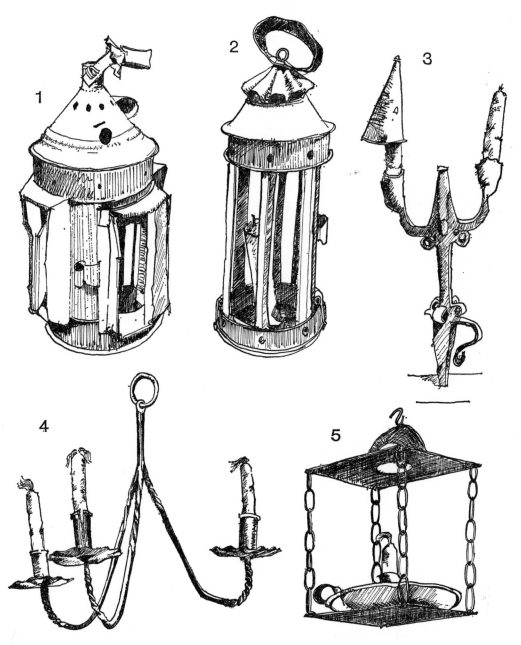

LANTERNS AND CANDELABRA. *From Filkins Museum*
*1, Shepherd's lanthorn. 2, Lantern. 3, Two-branch wrought-iron candle holder dug up in field.*
*4, Wrought-iron three-branch candelabrum made by the first Baptist minister at Filkins, who was also*
*a blacksmith. 5, Hanging brass candleholder.*

sweating come next, and then black heat, the one which gives the matt lustre to the forged metal such as one sees on parts of a waggon and is used for springs when too great a heat would destroy their elasticity. Warm heat, the most moderate, gives no glow to the metal but is still hot enough to burn the fingers, as many an apprentice discovered in days of old.

In recent years there has been another revival in wrought-iron work, which declined after the closing of the Gimson workshops. Such things as gates, sets of fire-irons, brackets and grilles keep alive an ancient art that came to full flower in medieval times, when the work of craftsmen making necessary articles such as hinges and iron bands on church doors, closing rings, candelabra and hanging brackets for lamps was both decorative and useful. At Duntisbourne Abbots, a village at the head of the Dun valley, a fifteenth-century smith finished off the church door with a closing ring as good to look at today as when it was first wrought (Pl. 127), and at Syde, a few miles distant, another ring of the same period suggests the same smith may have wrought both pieces. Both these churches are situated in hamlets hidden away at the top of steep narrow valleys running into the hills, the churches small and the fabric resembling the farm buildings around them. Look at any church door whose ancient timbers are held together by ironwork and one sees that the blacksmith was rarely content with plain bands but extended bands and hinges across the door, splaying out the ends into simple leaf-like shapes to give them grace as well as strength.

Village blacksmiths were sometimes clock-makers, the making of timepieces having always fascinated the worker in metal. In Ebrington Church there is a face-less clock two or three hundred years old which still chimes the hours. Tom Chadwick the artist, going into the tower to draw the works, told me it looked as if it had been made largely out of parts of an old cider-press. It is not known who actually made it; tradition says it was the village smith who lived beside the smithy now translated into a residence. We know the clock was in existence in the middle of the eighteenth century because entries in the churchwardens' account books show money was paid 'for oyle and new ropes' as well as a yearly sum for cleaning and overhauling paid to various Ebrington blacksmiths down the years. The original weight, a large battered cylinder of stone worn at the base by friction each time it hit the floor, was replaced by another stone weight, a more elaborate one with a touch of ecclesiastical-type carving about its shoulders, and this also was discarded for an iron weight which is still used today.

The clock has to be wound up every day by hand, the winder climbing the narrow stone stairs so hollowed by the wear of ages that each step must be carefully negotiated. A woman who during the last war undertook to wind it when

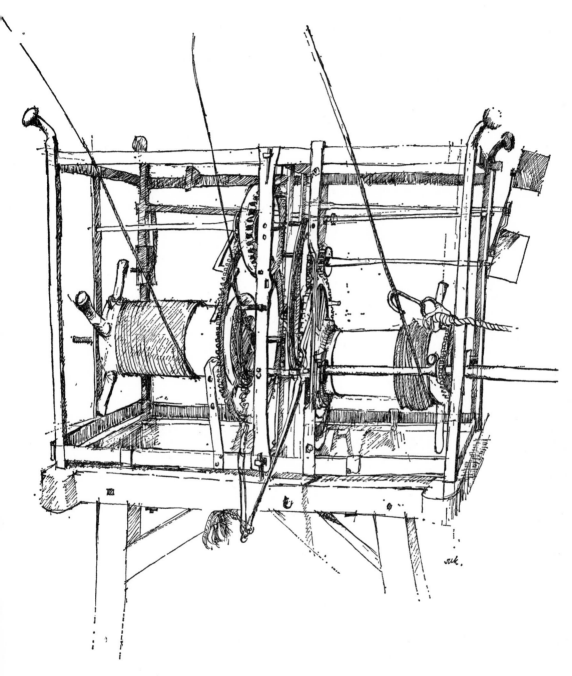

*Ebrington's faceless church clock.*

there was a shortage of men told me she used to regulate it with a piece of match-stick and that she calculated the time by counting a ring of horse nails, the two inches of space between them representing five minutes. It has a crown escapement and in its original form was exceedingly heavy to wind but an enthusiast modern-ized the winding mechanism. Otherwise it is unchanged. It looks an extraordinary collection of ropes, wheels and pulleys to the uninitiated, and has an oil consump-tion as heavy as that of an old car, but for the last two and a half centuries at least it has served the people of the village, a memorial to a village craftsman more lasting than his tombstone.

# The Plough

THE earliest form of plough and one that has been in continuous use on Cotswold since Saxon times is the breast plough, an implement a man propels by his own strength and without the aid of oxen or horse, cutting the ground and turning the sod; an arduous task even for a strong man. A modern version, that is with an iron share instead of one of wood, is still used occasionally by smallholders cultivating a grassy slope whose steepness makes it impossible to use any other kind of implement, though the small motor-driven Rotovator will soon have taken its place if it has not already done so. Thomas Hennel said that 'till the end of the nineteenth century it was not uncommon in Gloucestershire for eight to ten men to be employed on a field together, pushing the blades under the surface to a depth of two or three inches'. As the usual depth of soil on a hill farm was rarely greater than this the breast plough would be reasonably efficient for the job. It was heavy on man-power, but in the days of surplus cheap farm labour this would not be a serious consideration.

The breast plough consisted of a stout handle from six to eight feet long, with a downward curve towards the blade end, the two ends of the handle or beam morticed into a cross piece broad in the middle and with a rounded handle on each side. The blade, about a foot long and sixteen to eighteen inches wide, had a flange on the left side turned up at right angles by which the edge of the slice was cut. The beam was fixed in the socket of the blade by a wooden wedge. A man using a breast plough had to protect his thighs, and pieces of tough horse-hide with strips of wood fastened lengthwise to them provided the usual protection (Pl. 138). By pushing his thighs against the cross-handle and using his weight he forced the blade along a couple of feet at a time.

A primitive form of plough used by men on their allotments was a kind of shovel made by the local smith. It had a short handle and a wide, curved cutting blade turned slightly upward fastened on the thick stick, which had a natural curve near the socket. The worker pressed with the inside of his right knee, protected by pieces of sacking tied with string, against the back of his hand to get a purchase each time he cut a slice. This tool was sometimes used by roadmen for turf cutting, and also by the wheelwright's apprentice to cut the sods placed round the ring of fire for heating tyre wheels. Most countrymen in those days had an eye for a bough or piece of timber with a natural curve to use for tool handles, and when one was found it was put by for future use. The village carpenter kept a stack of such timber.

By the middle of the eighteenth century the boom in farming was encouraging investors to turn their skill to new types of agricultural implements and machinery, and as it became increasingly easier to produce them in standard types, ploughs made by local blacksmiths were often superseded by those bought from dealers in farm machinery. Hand-made ploughs, though often better suited to a particular farm or district, like any other hand-made commodity, could not be produced quickly enough or in sufficient numbers and demand rapidly overran supply.

As ploughs became more intricate in structure the ordinary smith who, using hand bellows, could undertake only wrought-ironwork, bought cast-iron shares and turn-furrows from the country foundries, small establishments who used the water-wheel to work furnace-bellows. These foundries, many of ancient origin, were yet another rural industry operating on the banks of streams and rivers which had to succumb to the competition of steam-power. As in the cloth mills, the output was determined by weather and a long drought could bring production to a standstill. Since these were small family concerns without much capital they found it impossible to compete with firms specializing in farm implements and machinery who had modern plant in industrial towns.

Not all local smiths and foundries were absorbed into the modern pattern. A few highly skilled craftsmen and individualists whose work meant more to them than big profits survived well into the twentieth century. The quality of their work, the stubbornness of a few farmers who appreciated it, kept them in being. Such a man was John Savery of Earthcott, in Gloucestershire, born of a long line of plough-makers famous in the district, who continued to make ploughs in his smithy till he retired. A story is told of a champion ploughman who won prizes with a Savery plough against men using the finest commercial products: 'Make I a plough, and do'e take extra trouble over en, for I've got plenty of meny to pay for 'en, and I'll take and plough the whole world with your plough.'

There were many new publications describing the new methods and machinery coming into use, as well as the catalogues of the makers of the new implements to tempt the farmer to change his old ways: Jethro Tull's *Book of Husbandry* and Thomas Hale's *The Complete Body of Husbandry*, for general information, and Rudge, William Marshall and others dealing with Gloucestershire. Farming had become big business and the way to prosperity was to keep abreast with new ideas and methods.

The landed gentry on their estates, the large farmers and the small—and from the seventeenth century onwards there have always been more large farmers than small on Cotswold—were interested in the new science now the Enclosures had made progressive farming possible.

Ploughing matches instigated by Agricultural Societies were more than entertainment and encouragement to farmers and their ploughmen, they helped the inventors working to improve the plough. On the ground they could see the implements of their competitors as well as their own in action by the most competent ploughmen, while the farmers could assess the various types; in the old days a ploughing match was good publicity for new types of plough. Messrs Ransome, for instance, kept a team of horses and two ploughmen to compete in ploughing matches all over the country and so learned the needs of different localities and types of soil by practical experiments.

The breast plough, however, continued to be used throughout the century. Rudge, writing in 1800, says it was common on Cotswold for preparing the ground for turnips, a crop providing winter feed for cattle, a great break-through from the old way of killing off most of the animals because of the scarcity of winter feed. Rudge mentions that the old type of plough, with one wheel and shortened beam, was the one mostly used on Cotswold and that four horses using a double-furrow plough could plough two acres a day on level ground. Rudge also mentions a Mr Radway of Cirencester, whose name is completely forgotten now like those of most local men who adapted implements to fit local conditions. The skill and ingenuity, in some cases the genius, of these now forgotten blacksmiths and the way they served their own localities cannot be overstressed. Although remote from the industrial centres where progress was proceeding with feverish and almost indecent haste to cash in on the new prosperity, the country craftsmen nevertheless were affected by the surge of new knowledge flooding the workshops of Britain. Cotswold had its own mechanical geniuses—Jonathon Hull of Campden who invented a steamboat and a new kind of slide-rule, Charles Keyte of Snowshill who invented an early form of sewing machine, Isaac Warner of Campden who made a set of chimes for the bells of Campden church, and the blacksmith who made Ebrington's faceless clock.

Rudge gives two ploughs invented by Mr Radway for special use on Cotswold. A skim-plough with a share thirteen to fourteen inches wide which turned over the turf completely, and a skim-and-go-deep plough that pared off the turf, covered it with four inches of earth and moved with one wheel. After the ploughing, a scuffler or drag, which had tines flattened to an edge and was curved at the point, was used and this cut rather than tore, dividing the sod into small pieces. It was very useful on light soil. Various kinds of scufflers are used today, particularly in districts where sprouts, cabbages and cauliflowers are grown extensively, such as the slopes about Campden and on the borders of Warwickshire and Worcestershire, and the name still persists. I saw it painted on a new large machine whose size and capacity and the way it was propelled would have amazed those eighteenth-century agriculturists.

As the eighteenth century came to a close, and well into the nineteenth, the small local makers of farm machinery became absorbed into big firms who took over old patents when there were any and became the sole source of manufacture. Ransome's of Ipswich had the ploughs.

Long after the breast plough had ceased to be used on the farm it continued to be used on allotments or 'lands' by cottagers who planted wheat to supply their households with flour for bread, reaping it with a hook and threshing it with a flail and then taking the corn to be ground into flour by the local miller. Several elderly men I have talked with remember doing this in their younger days, and described the whole process from seedtime, when the corn was put in with a dibber one grain at a time, to eulogies of the bread made from their homegrown wheat. At Ebrington and many another village the bread was baked in a communal oven, the miller often being baker as well, and I have been told many times how sweet was the smell of this bread and of its nutty taste and heavy texture so that a slice spread with lard flavoured with rosemary was a meal to be remembered with nostalgia.

This form of breast plough was also used for potato planting in small fields and allotments. Margaret Westerling in *Country Contentments* gives an example in 1939 from Calcot, a village near Bibury. It was made by the local smith and had a beam from five to six feet long of tough dry ash, rising to the coulter hole and becoming nearly horizontal towards its forward end; an ungainly-looking implement and needing considerable strength to propel.

# The Flail

IN ancient times the flail was combined with the sickle as a symbol of harvest and it has had continuous use until recent years on Cotswold, for when flails became obsolete on the farm with the coming of the threshing machine they continued to be used by men who grew corn on their allotments, lingering on well into the 1930s in remote villages until it was no longer possible to find a working mill to grind the corn or faggots cheap enough to heat the old-fashioned ovens in which the baker and cottager baked their bread. Old flails can still be found in sheds and outhouses, mostly with the leather or eelskin thongs perished by damp or vermin. Under the dust and cobwebs one can still see the smoothness of the handle polished by the sweaty hand of the thresher, and the swingel burnished by contact with the shining grain.

The handle, the longer of the two sticks which make up the implement, was usually made of ash, like so many handles of farm tools; the shorter stick, the swingel, is the part which strikes the straw to shake out the grain. The two are hinged together by a piece of split ash nicked and bent over the top of the stick and bound closely to it, the two ends joined together with a thong of tough pigskin, leather or, on the older flails, eelskin. The hinge is known as a shuckle in north Cotswold. The joining of the two sticks called for careful measurement; if the join were too loose the thresher could, as one old man told me graphically, swinging a stick to show me the movement, 'bring it down on yer 'ed'. He remembered doing this at his first attempt and had never forgotten how painful it was.

Another type of joint was a kind of ball and socket arrangement which allowed movement in any direction. A wooden cap was fitted at the top of the stick and tied to the swingel by a loose but intricate knot made of leather or eelskin. Tusser recommends holly or blackthorn for the swingel, but actually any hard wood was used, yew and blackthorn being the favourites. Men usually made their own flails or collected the parts and asked a fellow worker who was an expert to assemble them, for there were always experts in the small special skills needed on a farm in those days and as I have been told many times it was taken for granted that one should help the other. By the middle of the nineteenth century flails could be bought at shops dealing in agricultural implements but a good thresher preferred his own as fitting more comfortably into his hand and being of the right weight to suit his action. It was used with a circular action which was easier for keeping up a steady rhythm, and unless properly made and properly handled it could act like a boomerang and strike the user instead of the grain.

Threshing with a flail was monotonous, gruelling work. I have never met a man yet who said he enjoyed it, though many have told me they enjoyed ploughing, hoeing, reaping and stooking. Threshing was winter work when it was impossible to get on the land, but though the temperature might be below freezing outside the men threshing in the barn perspired freely. As the doors of the barn were left open for the draught to winnow the grain they were assailed at the same time by a cold wind as well as being choked by the chaff and dust from broken straw.

The monotony was made endurable because it was done in a small team, five or six threshing on the floor together. They could not sing at their work, the dust and the effort made it impossible, but they could work together beating out rhythms. I was told about one group of men who were also bellringers and who when threshing followed the same rhythms as when ringing the bells; as they were accomplished change-ringers this must have been quite a feat. Their master was also a bellringer and he would listen as he went about his work in the cattle yard. On one occasion the sound was being continually disrupted and on entering the barn he discovered that a new man who had taken the place of one who was sick, was not a bellringer. The other men were trying to show the newcomer how to follow their rhythms. The man was promptly told by his master to become a bellringer, and such was the authority of the farmer in those days that the man accepted the ruling without objection.

In the bad times of the late nineteenth century relief officers arranged with farmers to pay part of the wages of men given work threshing to reduce the burden on parish relief. The job was poorly paid, like all manual labour. In some districts the flail was known as the 'poverty-stick' and one old farmer I asked about this said he remembered as a boy his father's caustic remarks about this kind of labour. Often the men did not have the strength or the will to do the work properly and without a foreman driving them it was badly done.

# 3

# THE CROPS AND STOCK

*'The best citizens spring from the cultivators.'*

# Sowing the Seed

THE many kinds of seed-drills invented throughout the nineteenth century put an end to broadcast sowing. At first local inventors, mainly blacksmiths and carpenters, were inspired by the farming revolution to produce devices to suit local needs and then towards the end of the century these were taken over by big engineering firms to become standardized and factory made. The old methods, however, prevailed long after new machinery was available, particularly when a farm was split into small units to provide for a number of sons and there was little spare capital for machinery.

An early device called a Fiddle was supposed to ensure an even sowing of seed. The seed flowed into two cups which were whirled round. A bowstring was looped on a spindle and as it was drawn backwards and forwards the seed was thrown out by centrifugal impulse. It needed less skill by the operator and the seed was thrown out on both sides. Another device was the seed-barrow which had a long hopper laid across a simple wooden frame, two legs and a largish wheel in front. Both of these were very little improvement on hand-sowing except that they could be operated by less experienced workers. Jethro Tull's seed drill was one of the earliest to be used extensively for it was taken up by progressive landowners, and they also used his horse-hoes long before the smaller farmer could afford them. These implements were drawn by one horse, the operator following holding the handle of the chassis, where he could see the seed in the hopper and fill again when necessary. A strip of brass controlled by a screw was used to adjust the size of the outlet and so regulate the amount being cast.

Broadcasting seed goes back to the beginning of husbandry; one cannot but think of the parable of the sower. The seed was carried in a seed-cot, a large kidney-shaped container (Pl. 142), basket or box, slung at the left side of the sower, and he threw it with his right hand as he walked across the field, throwing it high and wide before him at each step until the opposite side of the field was reached. When he turned, the seed-cot was pushed round to his right side and he threw the corn with his left hand. The art was to keep an even stride and his eye on the stick set up at the headland to guide his course. On Cotswold, where many of the fields are on rising ground, another stick was placed between the two to keep his course straight.

The seed-cot was generally made of thin wooden boards bent to the required shape so that it fitted on the hips. An experienced sower could regulate the amount so as to let fall the correct quantity of seed required for each acre. Seed corn was precious and the work was given to a trusted worker, and a sower must have always been conscious that when the seed began to sprout and show above ground there would be evidence of his skill as a sower. Seed sown in furrows became common after the publication in 1733 of Jethro Tull's *Horse-Hoeing Husbandry*, which pointed out the advantages of keeping the crop free from weeds by hoeing between the rows.

When the seed was sown on the furrow it was essential to harrow it in as soon as possible to protect it from rooks and other birds which followed the sower, as the parable tells us. Many a small boy or girl spent lonely and chilly hours in the fields bird-scaring for a few pence a week, armed with a clapper made of two boards, a couple of pebbles in a tin, or only their voices and hands to keep the birds off the corn. At Winchcombe the pay was twopence a day or a penny and one swede, according to Eleanor Adlard.

Mrs Casey of Starveall who died in 1971 aged ninety-two, remembered the misery of her bird-scaring days until she died and though I heard the story many times her terror of those vast lonely fields and of the voracious and seemingly mocking birds came through with each telling. She was ten when she was first sent into the fields, the last of a family of eleven and the weakling.

'How my legs used to ache and my chilblains burn! The rooks laughed at me. They'd go on poking in the ground till I got almost up to them, and then they'd look so big and black and wicked. I never saw crows as big as those in Mister Fisher's fields. One day I was so tired I sat down and let 'em be. Farmer came by on his horse and gave me a cut with his whip for being idle, so I ran home and told my mother and showed her where the whip had cut my legs. I wouldn't go bird-scaring no more so I was sent over to Moreton to learn the dairying, my Aunt Polly was head dairymaid at the big house. I was so afraid I'd be sent back I tried my best. That's how I came to be head dairymaid and I won several prizes for my butter and Missis was pleased, I can tell you. That's how I met Fred, he was starting up on his own, and I had my own dairy with a couple of cows.

'I swore none of my children should have to go bird-scaring and they never did. When prices was bad we managed food for them, milk and skim-milk cheese and potatoes and a bit of bacon from the pig . . . And we managed . . . the little 'uns would go cressing in the brook and earn a penny or two selling them, Bill and

Joe worked at the kennels, and Jenny helped old Mrs James in her shop. She didn't get much money but we got our groceries a bit cheaper . . . it's wonderful what you can do when you set your mind to it.'

# Haysel

CONTRASTING the old methods of hay-making with the new it is easy to see the old ways in a rosy haze, forgetting the toil and sweat, the wet summers when the cut grass rotted in the fields and the long hours in the fields, and remembering only the bloom and freshness of early summer, the larks overhead, the men with scythes working in formation across the sweet-smelling meadows, the women in white aprons and sunbonnets following behind with their long wooden ellrakes. Nevertheless, hay-harvest pleased not only the sentimentalists from the towns, the Victorian artist looking for a picturesque scene for his canvas, but the countryfolk who did the work. Talk with any elderly countryman and one realizes that for the most part this was a season of joyous labour in the fields.

There was more than one reason for this. It meant a little extra money, always welcome in those days of large families and small wages, and it was a community effort: not only the farmworkers were involved but also their women and children, and in many instances practically the whole village turned out to help, those who worked at other jobs during the day turning up in the evenings to lend a hand. Though they worked from dawn to dusk there was time to exchange a joke or gossip in the breaks for meals, and other opportunities when the scythe blades were being sharpened on the 'rubbers' carried in a leather loop at the back of the mower's belt. It was necessary to do this at short intervals for a blade soon lost its sharpness on the tougher grass stems and it was not a job to be hurried.

A good mower reckoned to cut an acre a day on the flat, but on a Cotswold hillside this called for greater effort. A man who slowed down was soon called to order by the leader of the gang. Once he got into the rhythm there was pleasure in the movement and pleasure for the beholder in the curve of the blade and of the body, and the crisp swathes falling.

At meal times, sitting in the sun if the wind was chill or under a wall for shade if the sun poured down, aching muscles were forgotten as the women gossiped and the men told tales and joked. It was a long day. Breakfast at six, lunch at half-past nine, dinner at noon, an afternoon break at four o'clock and then supper at seven.

Sometimes the women would make a fire to boil a kettle for tea, and in the drowsy afternoon hour when energy flagged the farmer's wife, anxious to encourage the workers, would bring jugs of tea and home-made cake, and then it became a feast, and everyone lolled and ate and drank and returned to work refreshed. There was plenty of cider. The barrel was set up in the field and the men could refill their little wooden barrels or stone jars as often as they pleased. Free food and drink were often the only payment for casual helpers.

As evening fell the talk died away and they worked quietly, doggedly, forcing the last ounce from tired muscles and aching limbs, watching the sky for portents of next day's weather. It if promised fair then the hay could be left as it had fallen or raked into rolls, but threats of rain meant it must be raked into cocks so that the water ran off quickly. If the weather was set fair they need not work far into the gathering dusk. The constant preoccupation of a farmer in those days was the weather; a good farmer must do all he could to win the continual battle between his work and the elements.

On hillsides too steep for a cart or waggon a kind of low home-made truck was used to bring the hay down to the rickyard, or the nearest flat ground. This had a pair of axles and four small wooden wheels. A more primitive sled, a framework of rough timber on wooden runners, was used for carrying not only hay but fallen timber—dead wood for firing—through a woodland ride or through lanes deep in snow, pulled by a horse or by men with ropes. I watched one bringing home great boughs from a dead tree over a field covered with snow one Christmas morning near Chipping Campden and noticed that the framework was fastened with strips of hide. It was explained to me that nails would soon shake out as the sled 'wombled' so over rough ground.

Mowing machines, swathe-turners or tedders, mechanical rakes of every description, elevators first driven by horses and then by motors, all these rather fearsome looking machines dangerous in the hands of the inexperienced have taken the place of the men with scythes, the women with the long wooden rakes, the primitive sweep of 'tumbling Jack', as it was called. This contrivance was used for carrying hay not from the cocks but from the rows of raking after the cocks had been carried. It varied in different places but the usual form was a beam with spikes sticking out before and behind and drawn by two wires and guided by a boy. The spikes slid beneath the hay to collect it and when full it was drawn to the rick and there the driver pressed down the handles so as to push the front spikes into the ground, making the machine turn right over and leave a pile of hay behind.

It is almost impossible to say when the various mechanical devices for building a rick, before elevators became common, came into use. On farms whose fields were sloping, men continued to use scythes until well into the twentieth century. Some farms, with perhaps one mowing machine, went on in the old way until they turned over to silage, building their ricks with three men armed with 'shuppicks'. One stood on the waggon, another halfway up the ladder while a third stood on the top of the rick and arranged the load, the most important part of the job and given to the most experienced man, for a season's hay could be lost if the rick was badly made, and the workmen themselves were the first to criticize a badly made rick, pride in their own work including the right to criticize others. When the elevator became popular the job was done more quickly and with less back-aching labour, one man feeding the elevator and two men at the top of the rick taking the hay off the moving platform and stacking it. It was a dusty, thirsty job, the particles of dried seeds and grass filled the nostrils and mouth until they were parched. The man in charge reckoned to have his gallon jar of cider refilled at each break during rick-making. Albert Rastall, a farm worker all his life, told me how he used to start at haysel and corn harvest at four in the morning and always had at least a gallon of cider before breakfast at seven-thirty and so on during the day. And when food was brought to the fields it was 'good tack', home-made bread, fat bacon, 'as much as you could eat'.

The scythe men went in gangs and always used their own scythes, taking them to the blacksmith's to be 'hung'. 'A good scythe and you didn't know you was using it.' They worked from early morning until eight o'clock in the evening, later if they wanted to finish before the weather broke. I asked Mr Rastall if the long hours were exhausting.

'It wasn't all rush and bustle like it is today and you was never short-handed. There was always someone to help, might be only a boy. You worked steady but not so as to kill yourself and you didn't want to rush off to do something else like today; work was your life.' And he added, as many other elderly farm workers have done when talking about the old days: 'We didn't earn much but they was happy days. We were happier than they are today, I reckon. There was always something to look forward to.'

124–126. *Blacksmiths' work. Top, roasting trivet from Quenington, showing the underside. Centre, well bucket used to draw water at Oakridge Lynch. Below, 'ice creepers' made in 1957 by the late Mr Davis, blacksmith of Bisley.*

127. *Late medieval closing ring on the church door, Duntisbourne Abbots.*

128. *Wrought-iron gate, Chalford, made for his house by Richard Chew, blacksmith, incorporating his initials and those of his wife, Elizabeth.*

129. *Detail of drainpipe, Rodmarton Manor; design of Norman Jewson.*

130. *Wrought-iron gate by the local smith, School Lane, South Cerney.*

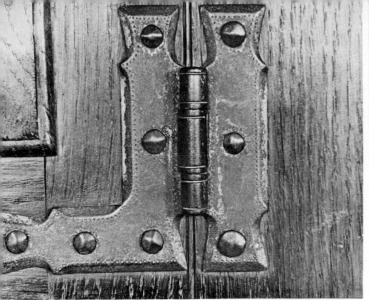

133. *Handle made by Alfred Bucknell; on a writing table.*

134. *Library fireplace. Screen by F. Baldwin; steel fender by F. Baldwin and his son; roasting fork designed by E. W. Gimson and made by F. Baldwin junior.*

COTSWOLD REVIVAL; RODMARTON MANOR.

131. *Steel hinge by F. Baldwin.*

132. *Fastener made by Edward Barnsley; on a bookcase.*

135. *Drawing-room fireplace. Fender by F. Baldwin; 'dogs' and fire-irons by Alfred Bucknell.*

136. *Ploughing match at Ebrington,* 1900.

137. *Spring ploughing at Springer's Farm, Rodborough, in the* 1940s. *From a photograph by the late W. H. Adams.*

138. Mr R. Soule demonstrates the 'breast plough' used by himself and his father. It is propelled by the thighs, which are protected by a special pad.

139. 'Skim-and-go-deep' plough by Larkworthy of Worcester. From Chavenage, in the collection of Mr R. Soule, Southrop.

140. *Ransome plough used at Meysey Hampton. Collection of Mr R. Soule.*

141. *Horse hoe used by Mr A. Twinning, Quenington.*

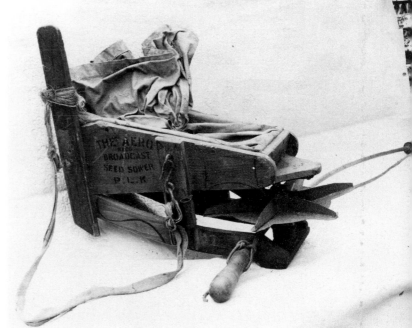

142. *Seed-lip for broadcasting seed; held on the hip. Old Court Farm, Lower Stone.*

143. *Seed-fiddle used by the late Harry Steel at Home Farm, Selsley.*

146–147. *Harrowing and rolling, Stringer's Farm, Rodborough, in the late 1940s. From photographs by the late H. W. Adams.*

144–145. *Mr A. Twinning demonstrates the seed drill. Below, showing the mechanism.*

148. *Hay Harvest at Stringer's Farm*, c. *1900. From a photograph by E. E. Hunt.*

149. *Unloading into a Dutch barn. From a photograph by the late H. W. Adams.*

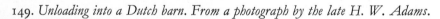

150. *Harvest: a family occasion at Callowell. From a photograph by the late H. W. Adams.*

151. *Harvesting at Callowell; raves in position on the waggon. From a photograph by the late H. W. Adams.*

152. *Rick-building, possibly at Callowell. From a photograph by the late H. W. Adams.*

153. *Mr C. Curtis of Bisley with a rick ornament.*

154. *Sail reaper, in the collection of Mr R. Soule, Southrop.*

155. *Hay knife; Southrop Manor.*

156. *Rick needle; inserted into the rick to test the temperature. Old Court Farm.*

157. *Hay-bond twiste Priory Farm, Leonar Stanley.*

158. *Riddle for clover seed; Priory Farm.*

159. *Barley hummeller, in Stroud Museum.*

160. *Gallon dry-measure, over a century old, used by Mr A. Twinning's grandfather at Quenington.*

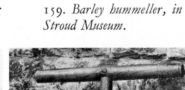

# Corn Harvest

THE significance of the corn harvest, once the most important festival of the agricultural year, has diminished during the last half-century even as the sheaves of corn high as a man which once took pride of place in the thanksgiving offerings made to the church Harvest Festival have diminished to a few ears or are not represented at all. Nowadays combine harvesters have done away with sheaves and stooks, and the making of decorative sheaf-knots to hold the binding of the sheaves together is a forgotten craft. In the old days when a good harvest was provision for the coming year everyone was involved, but now the fear of hunger has lost its bite and the rituals of harvest have faded away.

The first implements man used for reaping, the sickle, faggot hook and scythe, ancient as Father Time himself, have been superseded but a true countryman can still wield them in an emergency, and today when storms have laid the corn too flat for a combine or mechanical reaper to cut it men with scythes and sickles have been known to save the crop; so many centuries of inherited skill are hard to forget. Corn continued to be cut by hand well into the middle of the nineteenth century on large arable farms, and on the smaller farms until some fifty years ago, and later than that in a few instances. When farmers turned to machinery, allotment holders growing barley for the cottage pig or wheat for bread continued to reap with a sickle or faggot hook until conditions during the war years made it impossible to keep a pig, and the local mills which ground pig meal and flour for bread ceased working.

The sickle with its serrated edge was preferred to the heavier, smooth-edged faggot hook. Its sweeping curve, the result of centuries of experience, gave the tool a perfect balance, and although it was slower in action than the scythe, this was compensated by the fact that it did not need continual sharpening. A man worked himself into a natural rhythm for the series of movements, first the stooping and leaning forward to grasp in his left hand the straw near the ground, the pushing of the blade round it to draw it towards him and after each cut clearing the ears from the next handful, and when he could hold no more laying the bunch on one side by

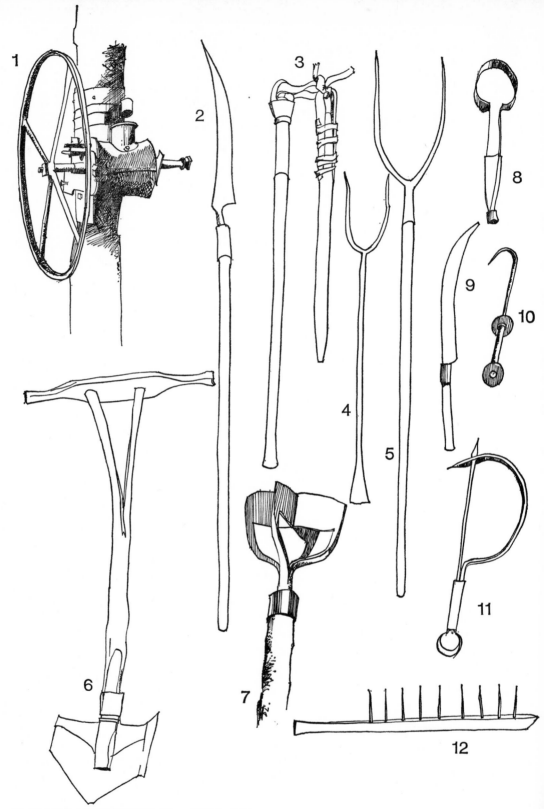

FARM IMPLEMENTS. *From Filkins Museum*
*1, Oat grinder. 2, Rick trimmer. 3, Flail. 4, 5, Pitchforks. 6, Breast plough. 7, Swede chopper.*
*8–12, Thatchers' tools.*

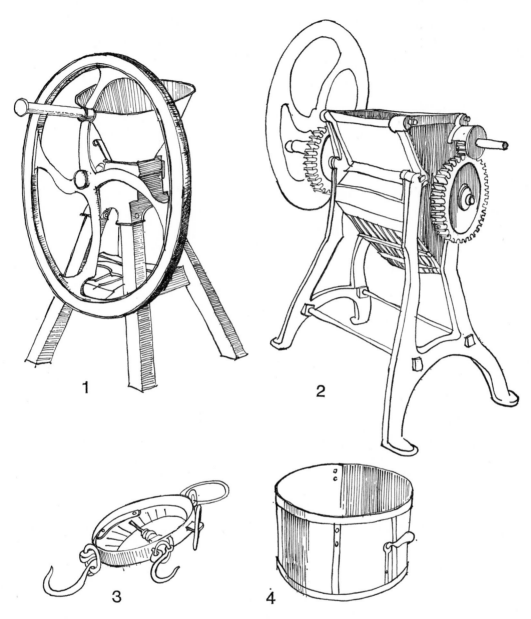

EQUIPMENT FROM TOWN FARM, EBRINGTON

*1, Bean mill. 2, Cake grinder. 3, Pig balance. 4, Tun pail.*

lifting it high over the standing corn with the ears supported in the curve of the sickle. To an onlooker it might seem slow at first, but watching each reaper's strip of about six feet gradually lengthening across the field as the hours went by and the gang worked steadily together one understood the reason for the unhurried rhythmical movements; the human frame could not endure the long hours of slogging except at a pace natural to each man's muscles. The binding of the sheaves was the work of the women and children. Albert Rastall of Ebrington told me he was given the job when he was ten years old and 'thought nothing of it'. There was one binder to three reapers and towards the end of the day the reapers laid down their tools and helped to set up the sheaves into stooks before going home.

Reaping with a scythe was more graceful to watch and entailed curving not bending the body, and when the reaping gangs used scythes these were fitted with a corn cradle which helped to lay the wheat in neat swathes ready for binding. Before harvest started the scythes were taken to the blacksmith's to be 'hung'. Each man had his own scythe and experience taught him how to adapt it to his own weight and height. The tool had to be adjusted so that it became part of the reaper, an extension of himself, and then the work was enjoyable. A man knew he looked well wielding a scythe, it gave him a dignity unlike any other task on the farm. Blacksmiths as well as reapers understood the necessity for making the tool fit the man, and one man told me he had walked eight miles to take his scythe to a particular blacksmith at Bourton on the Water because of his skill in setting scythes. It was this same old man, William Partridge, now dead, who told me that the only time in his boyhood that he received a whipping from his father that hurt was when he had borrowed his scythe to mow the churchyard. 'I was a grown man and in the team before I understood why he was so hard on me. You had to be jealous of your tools', he added.

Holidays in village schools were arranged to coincide with harvest times. The children's work in the fields was necessary as well as cheap. Everyone helped, even the shepherd who was generally considered free of duties outside his own. The corn must be harvested before it became over-ripe and everyone understood the urgency. Albert Rastall told me they sometimes worked on during the night if there was a moon, and the farmer's wife and daughters would bring food into the fields and there was unlimited beer and cider, the casks being set up in a corner of the field for the men to help themselves. The children led the horses and those whose fingers were too small and weak to tie the sheaves laid the straw rope about them to save the time of the woman or older child following on. Albert Rastall had a horn beaker for drink in the fields. It did not break when knocked over like a mug or a glass and it kept the drink cool. He had used it some fifty years and it was old when it came into his possession.

Straw rope for binding was made by a straw-rope binder or wimble, a crank like a brace but with a hook at the end where the bit is placed. Two people worked this device, one worked the crank and walked backwards, the other, after starting off the rope with a few strands looped on the hook, fed the straw into the twisting and lengthening rope. Some farms used bramble or briar trailers, George Swinford of Filkins told me, showing me a special bramble hook made by the local blacksmith for the purpose. The trails were run through a ring to remove the thorns and then made a good pliable binding. The knots varied in different districts. It is not easy to tie a knot in straw rope and it is almost impossible to describe this sleight of hand in words. When I have asked old men how they learnt to do it the answer has invariably been, 'When I was a little 'un', or 'I don't remember. We had to do it so we did.' Straw ropes and briars were also used to make bee skeps.

There was a school holiday for gleaning, or leasing, after harvest. Many cottagers depended on the wheat they gathered in this way and the corn grown on their allotments for bread during the year, especially when there was a large family of children, and without the gleaned corn many a child in those days would have gone

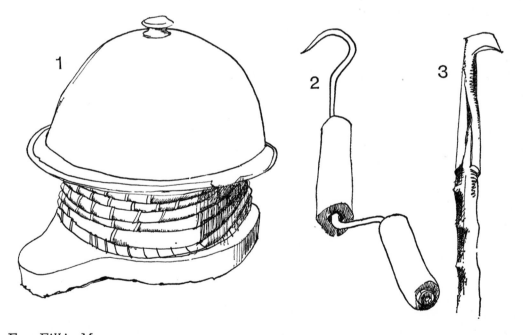

*From Filkins Museum*
*1, Straw bee skep made by George Swinford's uncle, with pot cover. 2, Straw-rope binder. 3, Bramble hook.*

without the slice of bread and jam at the dinner break. In some districts the church bell was rung at eight o'clock in the morning to tell the women and children when they could start, and in other districts a solitary stook was left standing to show gleaning must not begin until it had been carted away. In one village near Campden I was told with a bitterness still acute how one farmer kept the 'policeman', as this stook was called, until his wife and daughters had gleaned the field for corn to feed their hens. There was a story once told in the Plough Inn at Ford near the Guiting villages about a battle at Oak Piece at Temple Guiting. Going to the field after the church bell had rung—and they had been ready and waiting each morning with their sticks and bags—the women found that people from Stow were already leasing in the field. After a fierce encounter in which the sticks and bags as well as fists played a part, the Guiting women drove off the intruders until they ignominiously ran home. The story of this ancient battle through the years became a tale told with jest and laughter but at the time, though there was probably enjoyment of a kind for the participants, it was as hard fought as any battle for the rights of man, and unlike many such battles ended with the defeat of the invaders.

The Harvest supper was the one occasion when the farmer, his family, with the vicar and any of the local gentry who cared to participate, served the workers including the blacksmith, wheelwright and as many other tradesmen or outsiders as might be said to have had a connection with the harvest—and if it had been a good one and the farmer was a kindly man then he was not too strict about this. Willing hands swept the barn, put up the trestle tables, brought in the barrels of beer and cider, laid the tables with cutlery, mugs and glasses and great platters of cut bread and cheese.

The farmer and his special guests sat at the top table, his womenfolk and maids waited on the tables, the others sat in order of importance, the foreman, the head carter, the shepherd nearest the top, the lesser men in order of seniority and descending to the farm boys at the bottom. This order was strictly kept by the workers themselves. The meal was of meat, roast beef or mutton, with great dishes of roast and boiled potatoes and greens, and, to follow, apple pudding or plum duff which had been boiled in the copper; bread and cheese filled in the corners. And after the food, mugs freshly filled with beer or cider and pipes lit, came the songs and the toasts and then the dancing.

One of the Harvest Homes still remembered twenty-five years after, and one of the last in the district, was at Ilmington, on the Warwickshire-Gloucestershire border. Sam Bennett, fiddler, folk dancer, 'the Last of the Troubadors' as John Bird called him in his booklet on Sam Bennett, was there to play for the dancing and the singing, taking part in both as he fiddled away in the old barn. They sang the customary 'Here's Health unto our Master' with the various workers, plough-men, carters, shepherds each singing their part. Sam, at the end, reciting 'The Farmer's Motto', a set of verses now forgotten.

*Let the Wealthy and Great*
*Live in Splendour and State*
*I envy them not,*
*I declare it.*
*I eat my own lamb*
*My own chicken and ham,*
*I shear my own fleece*
*And I wear it.*
*I have lawns, I have bowers*
*I have fruit, I have flowers*
*The lark is my morning alarmer,*
*So my jolly boys now*
*God speed the plough*
*Long life and success to the Farmer.*

# Winnowing

WINNOWING in its most primitive form is taking advantage of natural currents of air to separate the grain from the chaff. Before winnowing machines came into general use in the eighteenth century the winnower stood on a stool or block of wood in the barn between two open doors and shook the corn and chaff through a sieve held over a large piece of sail-cloth, the grain falling into the cloth and the chaff and dust blowing away. Long after it had been superseded by machines, allotment holders and small-holders used this method.

Grain being kept for seed went through several sievings or riddlings, first being shaken in a coarse riddle with a mesh of split cane or willow, and this brought most of the chaff to the top. The remainder was picked up by a wooden barn shovel to avoid bruising the grain and thrown across a current of air to fall into a heap on a newly-swept floor. The heavy grains remained in the centre of the heap and the 'tailings', the lighter poorer grain, fell to the outside and could be shovelled into separate containers.

While this method was adequate when farming was on a subsistence level, it was too slow when large quantities of corn had to be handled. The cleaner the grain the higher the price as well as the farmer's reputation on the Corn Exchange, once an important building in the nearest market town. One of the early attempts to improve the winnowing technique was a wooden structure with wide-spread heavy arms to which sacks were nailed, and when the arms were rotated by turning a handle a strong draught was created, blowing away the chaff and the dust. According to Sir Walter Scott this machine was introduced into Scotland from the Netherlands, but as the Cotswolds had had connections with the Netherlands since medieval times when Cotswold wool was sold there in vast quantities this machine may have reached the Cotswolds direct.

Sid Knight, in *Cotswold Lad* (1960), describes the winnowing machine used in his grandfather's time at Broadway as 'a metal, box-like contrivance of the size and shape of the old Italian barrel-organ', and this was probably the machine known as the Blower. It was operated by three men and was still in use on small farms at the end of the nineteenth century. It consisted of a hopper with five fans fixed to a spindle in the centre turned by a cranking handle. One man fed the grain into the hopper, another turned the handle, a third carried away the dressed corn. The machine was placed with its tail to the open barn door so that the draught helped to carry away the chaff. Sieves of various sizes to suit the kind of grain being cleaned could be put into the Blower.

The bushel, the standard measure for grain, was a circular wooden drum strengthened with metal bands with two iron handles about halfway down the drum. A special stick went with it for levelling off the top when the bushel was filled. Filling the bushel was a precise job, usually superintended by the farmer or his foreman because if packed down too firmly more than the correct amount would be measured. It had to be lightly poured in and then, in the case of wheat, the heaviest grain, the stick drawn across lightly. For lighter grain it was drawn across in zig-zag fashion. Carters helping themselves to their allowance for their horses had to be watched carefully, though as Albert Rastall told me 'there was always ways of getting an extra handful'. Carters liked their teams to look sleek and glossy and a few extra handfuls of oats could make all the difference; a carter with a team of shiny-coated horses could hold his head high when he met another team.

On some farms threshers were made to empty their boots before going home, for a certain amount of grain fell into them as they worked and sometimes a little more was added to feed the cottage pig, poultry or children in bad times when bread was dear. Some farmers even made it a condition of employment that their workers did not keep a pig, because of the risk of pilfering; the bins and over-flowing sacks must have been a constant temptation when wages were below subsistence level and their masters getting high prices for their corn.

## THE BARLEY HUMMELLER OR AWNER

Cotswold has always grown as much barley as wheat, if not more, the nature of the soil suiting the crop. Often it was grown for malting, and this in the eighteenth century when bread and corn were scarce caused riotings around Gloucester by men who saw grain being sold for making beer when it should have been used for feeding the hungry. Malting barley has to be of a high standard, and when the crop was poor quality much of it was fed to pigs and poultry. As the beards or awns of the barley were injurious to them most farms had a barley hummeller. This was a hand tool consisting of a kind of iron grid with a long handle, the parallel bars of the grid sharpened underneath. It was beaten down lightly on the barley to remove the awns (Pl. 159). Another type had a short stick—the handle—with a set of blades about an inch apart set vertically in parallel bars and it was dropped with a chopping movement on the barley. Awning was an unpopular job, for the awns had a way of travelling about inside the clothing, pricking and irritating the skin, while one up a nostril, in the mouth, ear or eye could be very painful.

A mechanical barley hummeller took the form of a wooden trough raised a little higher on legs on the end nearer the crankwheel, which turned a spindle holding the cutters inside. There was a small spout at the low end and at the other a wide shallow hopper into which the barley was placed. Many of these mid-nineteenth-century implements and machines were still being used until the last war, though modern types were available. When the firm who made them no longer supplied the old model or parts for them, or if there were changes of management on a farm, then new machines and methods might be instituted, but a characteristic of Cotswold farmers is a strong conservatism and as long as an implement did its job and there was sufficient labour it continued in use.

# Special Crops

TEAZLES

WHEN the cloth trade got under way in the south Cotswolds at the beginning of the eighteenth century tremendous numbers of the burler's teazle, *Dipsacus sativus*, were required, yet strangely enough, the growing of teazles was usually undertaken by small farmers with family labour willing to work long hours for a very chancy reward, or by labourers in other employment anxious to make a little extra money. They were grown in the flood basin of the Severn around Tewkesbury in vast quantities to supply the clothiers of the Stroudwater; others came from the Curry Rival district of Somerset and in addition large numbers were imported from the continent to meet the demand. They were still being grown near Cheltenham in 1939, according to the *Flora of Gloucestershire*, and I have been told of their being cultivated in the north Cotswolds near Cutsdean and Snowshill. Today they are no longer a commercial crop but one can still see them growing in Somerset. One grower I spoke to near Curry Rival told me his family came originally from Gloucestershire and had grown teazles there in the late nineteenth century.

The burler's teazle differs from the wild plant, *Dipsacus sylvestris*, by its spines or prickles, which are recurved, whereas these of *D. sylvestris* are straight and not hooked. The hooks of the burler's teazle attach themselves to the surface of the cloth and draw out the loose fibres and raise the nap as they are drawn across the cloth, without doing damage to its surface. It rarely naturalizes itself as a relic of cultivation. Dr Knapp, in his *Naturalist's Diary*, 1820–1830, noted that although the seeds were formerly swept from barns and teazle houses where the heads had been stored, and scattered in profusion in rubbish heaps where they vegetated freely, yet he never knew the plant to become established in the surrounding hedges. His Diary also contains records of its cultivation in the Thornbury area near Bristol.

The first record of its being grown in England was in the reign of Edward III, when the weaving of woollen cloth by Flemish weavers was established, the King having invited them to come to England and taking them under his protection. But cloth was being woven long before then, first the rough cloth of the peasantry (the nobles bought their cloth from the continent), and then as Weavers' Gilds were started in the twelfth and thirteenth centuries, material of finer quality, and this must have needed burling, probably by teazles imported from the great cloth-making country of Flanders.

The finishing processes were fulling, rowing and shearing, and the most import-ant of these was the rowing; that is, after fulling when the cloth was stretched on tenters to dry in the open air, the burler scratched the surface to remove loose knots and fibres and to raise a surface on the felted cloth. A shearer then sheared the nap smooth, the shears he used being the same kind as those used for shearing sheep but of finer quality. There are many representations of shears on woolmen's memorial brasses and carved in stone. Cranham church has two pairs carved on its tower, a mark of a former woolman or clothier who helped to raise the church.

Originally the teazle heads were set in a frame to form a kind of brush and the dresser worked by drawing it down the cloth, but as the cloth trade increased this process was too slow for the demand and the teazles were set in a revolving cylinder called a gig. The gig has changed little since the eighteenth century when the pro-cess, known as roughing or raising, was carried out in a handle house or dubbing shop instead of in the open air on racks. The handle house of an old mill can be recognized by small openings in the walls to allow free ventilation to keep the teazles pliable, for once they became dry and brittle the hooked prickles broke off and were useless.

While the clothiers of south Cotswold, particularly Wotton under Edge, im-ported teazles from Somerset, being on a direct road from Bristol where the teazles were sent to market, the Woodchester district grew many of its own teazles. It stored them in a tall round tower with latticed floors that is still standing. In wet seasons barns, sheds, shelters of every kind were used and the cottagers who grew a few patches of teazles often kept them in their bedrooms, an uncomfortable business for the occupants considering the nature of the heads and the large families who inhabited cottages in those days. No other means of raising the nap of cloth was invented for many centuries. In 1312 teazles were being grown in Gloucester-shire and sold at twopence a thousand heads, according to Anne Pratt, the earliest record for English-grown teazles.

Not all parts of the wolds are suitable for growing teazles; they like a heavy soil and if it is too light the hooks tend to be small or not to grow at all, but there is a capping of clay on many a hilltop and this is where the teazle fields were found. Dr Knapp said that a piece of cloth needed 150 to 200 'runnings up' with the teazle frame and in this process 1500 to 2000 heads would be broken, so it is easy to see why the cloth industry needed such vast numbers.

Rudge describes how, after sowing, the seeds are brushed in with thorns fastened to a hurdle, because the tines of a harrow would set the seeds too deep. At the beginning of June in the first year they are 'spittled' with a small spade or 'shoe', the surface soil carefully turned between each plant. Two months later they are 'grited', the earth turned up five inches and thrown to plants, and then the earth brought up around the plants with a hoe. The following spring they are 'grited' again to make them 'haddle out', or send out side shoots.

It can be seen that this kind of cultivation did not lend itself to mechanical farming and the larger farmers left teazles alone. In the first place the plant took two years to produce the heads and the fertility of the soil took a few years to return after a crop of teazles had been grown on it, though Rudge remarked on a field at Eastington just below Gloucester where teazles had been grown in the same field for over twenty years, but heavy manuring had been necessary. After the teazles had been harvested the field was often made ready for wheat as the weeding and manuring for the teazles were an excellent preparation for a corn crop.

A period of bad weather when the plant was coming into flower and two years' hard work of hoeing and hand weeding were wasted. It could bring a handsome profit in good years, though there never seems to have been a stable price; it increased if the weather was bad and the demand high, whereas a glut when there was a falling off in demand meant a low price. In 1815 King teazles fetched £4 a pack, in 1820 they had dropped to £2. Middlings soared to £8 a pack in 1821, only to drop to £4 in 1824 when the clothing mills were beginning to feel the competition from steam-powered machinery of Yorkshire. In the stock books of J. & T. Clark of Trowbridge £22 is recorded for one year, but this was exceptional, the average price being between £5 and £7.

The danger period for the grower is when the heads are almost ripe for picking. Just below the flower heads the shoulders of the long serrated leaves form a shallow cup which collects dew and rain. In fine weather this soon evaporates, but when the water stagnates in wet weather the stem and heads begin to rot and all hope of a good return vanishes. Ripe teazles cannot be stacked like corn because pressure damages the spines and a free circulation of air is necessary to dry them thoroughly. 'Bask them in any sunny gleam that breaks out', one experienced grower wrote, implying that the English summers of the early nineteenth century were not unlike our own.

Harvest time was the end of July and the beginning of August, just before the corn harvest. A special knife was used to cut the heads, and this had to be continually sharpened. The more quickly the harvest was gathered the easier it was, for once the stems lost their sap they toughened into a cane-like consistency difficult to sever. Bands of travelling cutters went from farm to farm during the teazle harvest in the same way as gangs of threshers and reapers; they brought their own tools and slept in barns and outhouses during the cutting season. A Wiltshire farmer in 1906 was advertising in a Bristol newspaper for cutters, which suggests he hoped to get men from the Bristol area (which would include Wotton under Edge), who might have finished local work and so could move on to Wiltshire.

The teazle heads were fastened to a pole for drying, thirty to a stave and thirty staves to a pole. The terminal heads from the centre of the top branch were ready first and, being larger and coarser than the others, were used for coarser cloth. These were called Kings and brought only about half the price of the collateral heads, the best of the crop known as middlings.

I have never been able to discover whether in the principal teazle-growing districts of Cotswold they had a harvest feast as they did in Somerset. An old record of a hundred years ago printed in *The Western Gazette* describes a meal laid on long tables, each table having a teazle basket as centrepiece filled with flowers, the heads of the teazles being outside and the stems woven to make the basket. It was called 'The Harvest Handful' or 'The King of the Teazles'.

Teazles had their own magic, like all plants which have been part of country life for centuries. Miss Plues, in her *Rambles in Search of Wild Flowers*, after commenting on the bundles of teazles she saw being prepared for market at a farmhouse in Vallis, Somerset, says: 'Country people cut open the heads where they frequently find a worm. Any odd number of these worms, placed in a quill, is believed to charm away sickness.'


PLANTS FOR DYES

*Woad.* A crop not grown on Cotswold for at least a hundred years is Woad, *Isatis tinctoria*, which was used for at least three centuries as a mordant or base for blue and black dyes and employed in the dyeing of the famous broad cloth made by the Stroudwater clothiers. Before ploughing subsidies encouraged farmers to plough every possible piece of marginal land woad could sometimes be found naturalized in out-of-the-way corners, the last vestiges of crops once grown in nearby fields, but today the only place where one might find a plant growing wild is on the Mythe, near Tewkesbury, where it has been recorded since 1818. Around Wotton under Edge, a town noted for its dyehouses in the early nineteenth century, it was once grown extensively, but with the introduction of indigo it fell from favour. Naturalized plants lingered on in the fields around Ithells Mill and Wickwar near Wotton until 1908.

Clothiers and dyers often grew their own woad, and at Stonemead, or Stean-mead, where the Townsends of Painswick had a large mill, we know it was grown because of a dispute about tithes about 1770, when the Vicar of Painswick believed tithes of woad should be paid to him because the Townsends were growing woad on land which had previously grown corn, rape and hay. This 'tythe hay grew on all such meads as had never been broken up . . . a meadow called Steanmead', and the matter was finally solved by a revisitation of all ploughed and unploughed land in the parish of Painswick in conjunction with the Impropriator in 1772: as a result the Rector received his tithes.

But this was not the first growing of woad in Painswick, for in 1615 tithes of woad were paid to Painswick church.

Wadfield or Woadfield is not an unusual field name on Cotswold. There is one near Sudeley and several in the south Cotswolds including a field called Woad Range at Saltford where a range of buildings stood in which woad was prepared for market. White's *Flora of Bristol* published in 1912 gives evidence of this by a botanist Mr D. Fry, who wrote: 'This I learned from C. Withers of Saltford, who told me he had often heard his father say that the plant was grown and the dye stuff made from it at Woad Range.'

An earlier record is a licence to grow woad granted by Elizabeth I in July 1590, to Richard Deverell and Valentine Harris for twenty years to sow a hundred acres of woad in each of the counties of Berkshire, Wiltshire and Gloucestershire for the annual rent of £50. This was a large sum in those days and the profits of woad-growing were considerable. A great quantity came from the Continent in the late Middle Ages, when Cotswold clothiers were selling their cloth to Bristol merchants for shipping abroad and in return buying, amongst other things, woad from Toulouse. As the clothiers produced more dyed cloth instead of sending abroad the undyed broadcloth, and the home market also increased, production of woad at home increased also. Any product depending on shipping in those days was apt to be lost by storms, pirates and other hazards, so clothiers whenever possible grew their own woad or encouraged local production.

In one of her journeys across the Cotswolds Celia Fiennes, who fortunately for the local historian was interested in everything she saw on her travels and wrote down her instant impressions, gives a good description of the making of woad, and it is very probable that she was describing the woad-mill on the Ey brook near Moreton in Marsh, recorded in the Victoria County History as working in 1656. To quote her: 'In the mill with a horse they grind the leaves into a paste, so make it up in balls and drye them in a Penthouse, to secure it from the rain, only the wind dryes it: a plantation of about twelve acres would employ two or three families, men, women and children, and so they generally come and make little huts for themselves for the season to tend it.'

Tending the crop and picking it was the pleasantest part of the job, making the woad the dirtiest and smelliest. The initial process was a paste made from the foliage of the plant, the leaves being picked three or four times at intervals of a few weeks; the first picking, being the most valuable, was kept separate from the rest. The leaves were first dried in the sun and then ground to a paste; it was sheltered from the rain until it fermented. When the fermentation was complete—usually in about two weeks if the weather was warm—the paste was moulded into flat cakes, sprinkled with water and left to ferment again. The final treatment was to mix the cakes with limewater to bring out the colour. The permanence and richness of the dye depended upon the number of fermentations, and this was the skilled part of the work. The fermentation produced a most offensive smell; the intrepid Celia Fiennes, who must have been accustomed to smells on her travels, remarked on it as do various writers of the period. The woad-makers were known by it for it pervaded their hair, their bodies and their clothes and local people were probably relieved when their work was done and they left the district, for woad-making was yet another of those peripatetic occupations which made the highways of England so full of life and colour in the old days.

The Dyers' Gild at Bristol regulated the sale and storage of woad coming into the port, and though a burgess of the city was legally entitled to break his own woad the regulations of the Gild controlled its sale and their own officers were appointed to break open the tuns or pipes in which it was stored. It is on record that *The George* carried an entire cargo of some 182 pipes from Bordeaux.

Woad was a difficult commodity, changing its potency if not properly handled. The Gild was well aware of this and their rules were strict. No merchant was allowed to store more than one tun at a time and merchants not of the city were obliged to sell their woad within forty days of an assay of its quality by the Gild, lest it began to perish after that time. They were also not allowed to sell dyestuffs to each other.

It is a charming plant, rather like a small shrub or bush and it is especially delightful at seed time when the pods wear a purplish flush, a hint of the dye it produces. Clusters of slender pods dangle on hair-like stems and tremble at the slightest movement of air. The tiny yellow flowers amongst the thin narrow leaves are irresistible to bees.

*Dyer's Rocket or Weld.* Weld, *Reseda luteola*, is a native limestone plant, not unlike *Reseda lutea*, the wild mignonette, but of a less shrubby habit and not so common.

The dye is prepared by making a decoction of the whole plant including the seeds which contain luteolan, a fast, strong, yellow dye. With the addition of alum many shades can be obtained.

It is one of the oldest known dyes, and is mentioned by Caesar as being used by the Gauls. Mixed with indigo, or in the old days with woad, it produced a colour known to Cotswold dyers as Saxon Green. When the south Cotswold clothiers began to manufacture cloth of other colours as well as their Stroud scarlets, Uley blues and black broadcloth to meet the demands of the expanding markets of the eighteenth century, they began to grow quantities of weld to increase the varieties of their coloured cloths. Rudge was much impressed by John Hawker's dyeworks at King's Stanley where 'seventeen furnaces were continually employed there and often forty-two pieces dyed in one day'. The dyeing book of the mill gives recipes and samples of its 'Rich French Grey, Pompodore Mixed, Rich Corbeau, Plumb Crimson, Light Blue, Olive and Eye White', to name but a few, and before the imports of logwood, redwood and cochineal from South and Central America much of the dyestuff came from locally grown plants.

Weld was often grown with barley as a catch-crop, for like woad it takes two years to mature, the first year's rosettes of leaves being left after the barley had been gathered to grow into mature plants the following year. It is a delicate-looking plant and in its wild state soon dies out in one place and then appears in another, often springing up in clearings and by the wayside where a road has been widened, its tall spires conspicuous because of the pale reseda of its leaves amongst the darker herbage around it. The seeds remain fertile in the ground for many seasons awaiting a favourable opportunity or the right depth of soil to germinate.

When cultivated it was pulled when the seeds began to form, tied in bundles and dried in the sun. These bundles were known as weldcord. As the plant begins to seed a soft russet tint spreads upward from the base and by autumn the whole plant takes on an orange glow not unlike the colour of the stone brash which is its favourite habitat. It can often be found in old quarries, the yellow of myriad small flowers on tall spikes almost lost in the yellowish green of its overall colour. Linnaeus observed that the flower spikes followed the sun.

According to a stock book of a Cotswold dyer 28 lb. of prepared Weld was worth 11s. 6d. in 1814, and Dr Perry says that 'as late as 1820 the plant was being sold in Bristol by country people at 10s. a hundredweight'. Probably these would be plants collected in the fields and hedgerows. It went out of favour because of the large amounts needed to produce the dye, though handloom weavers today who dye their own wool know its fast quality, the distinctive soft yellow far exceeding in aesthetic value the harsh yellows of commercial dyestuffs.

# Oxen

WORKING oxen were part of the Cotswold scene from early medieval times to the beginning of the twentieth century. Arthur Young records that bullock teams were as common as horses in 1760, and William Cobbett on one of his 'Rural Rides', in 1826, writing about winter wheat on the Cotswolds says, 'the ploughing and other work is done in great part by oxen, and here are some of the finest ox-teams that I ever saw'. Praise, indeed, from Cobbett who rarely had a good word to say about the Cotswold scene. But by the end of the eighteenth century the manufacture of lighter ploughs which could be drawn by two horses was already ousting the bullock teams of eight to twelve oxen needed to draw the early heavy ploughs, though on Cotswold the change-over came much later, only gradually infiltrating into hill farms. The large farms were probably the first to reduce their ox-teams; the smaller farmer and the more conservative found them cheaper to feed and easier to look after than horses, and although they were slower at work, when it was a family concern extra hours of labour did not mean extra expense.

It was the go-ahead farmer, the landowner, alive to new ways of saving time and money as well as wanting the prestige attached to owning a stable of splendid horses, who began the association of man working with horses on the farm. In the medieval world the heavy horses, ancestors to the shire horses, were kept to carry the nobility in their armour, but as the new techniques of farming developed the horse was bred for farm work. On the Cotswolds and downland counties such as Wiltshire and Berkshire oxen continued to be used for most of the heavy work on the land long after horses had taken over in other counties. They suited the light soil, their feet did less damage to the land, and they pulled with a steadier draught. They were less nervous than horses and more docile. In the early summer flies sometimes made them bolt, but the wise farmer saw that his beasts were dressed with some kind of fly repellant, and on most farms the ploughman or head carter had his own secret recipe for this which he made himself. Moreover, after they had been worked for a few years they could be fattened for beef, unlike the horse which when no longer fit for work was sent to the knacker's yard.

Their working day began at seven in the morning after they had been given a feed of hay, and went on until about four in the afternoon when they were watered and put out to grass. They needed no more attention until the following morning. They had two rest periods, like the man in charge of them, the first on reaching the ploughland and again at midday, when they chewed the cud while the ploughman ate his dinner. Ploughing with a double-furrowed plough they averaged an acre a day.

Ox-teams never received the same grooming and kind of decoration given later to teams of horses. When they pulled a farm waggon in a village festivity they might have a garland of wild flowers flung round their necks, but not for them the elaborate harness with its shining brass ornaments, the bells, the tails plaited with ribbons and straw. Perhaps the idea of dressing up an ox in fine harness and tinkling brasses seemed a little out of place, like dressing a village girl in the finery of a lady. The Bathurst oxen are the only oxen I know which had brass decorations on their collars, little brass knobs on the hames and a brass plate where the tug chain was fastened.

Oxen were docile and easy to handle but they could become 'clock conscious', as one old man who had worked with them in his youth told me. They knew when they had done their stint. When their usual time for stopping work came round nothing could induce them to go on working. This was recognized as a fundamental trait in the bovine character and accepted, whereas such obstinacy on the part of a horse and it would have been whipped. The goad was the only instrument of persuasion and this was only used to urge a lethargic beast to move a little more quickly. It was a nine-foot-long ash stick having at its tip a sharpened nail the length of a barleycorn, and the pattern of the goad remained the same from the beginning. Pictures from illuminated manuscripts such as the Psalter of Eadwine show the ploughman with the long goad in one hand while he guides the plough with the other, the goad reaching as far as the animals' heads. The tradition that the spike must be the length of a barley corn may have originated in those days. Its bulk and slow-moving brain saved the ox from the hard punishment given to disobedient horses. It was useless to punish an animal who could not understand why it was being punished.

The oxen broke themselves to harness. Hitched to a piece of timber they were left in the yard until they became accustomed to pulling it and to the collar about their necks. When an old pair were taken out of a team and a new pair had to be trained they would be placed in the centre of the team with an experienced pair before and behind; the master ox was placed on the off-side. The driver had his own calls for turning to left or right, which they recognized. When they worked in the harvest fields they sometimes had nets over their muzzles, but unless the harvest was very poor it was generally accepted that a few free mouthfuls were their share of the bounty of the season.

On the Springhill estate near Broadway oxen were used regularly until 1920. Mr Meadows, who had been in charge of this last team, still remembered their names with affection in 1938. Whitefoot and Dumplen were the leaders in a team of eight, then came Boxer and Spot, Rattler, Spider, Tinker, and Britton. They fetched sixty pounds apiece when they were sold with their harness 'to go to foreign parts'. One of the occasions remembered with pride by Mr Meadows was when the team pulled a Gloucestershire waggon to the fair at Stratford-on-Avon to carry the May Queen and her retinue, the oxen groomed, their harness polished.

The majority of oxen were cross-bred Herefords, the earlier ones were sometimes crossed with the Red Gloucester cattle. They made a fine picture with their massive heads and shoulders and great sweep of horns, some measuring three or four feet from tip to tip. Because of the stony nature of the ground and the farm tracks, and always when they were used for hauling, they were shod with small iron plates called cues, two on each foot. These are sometimes turned up in the fields today. Shaped rather like a half crescent, the straighter inner edge of the cue was placed along the inside of the cleft in the hoof, the narrow end turned up over the front of the toe and secured with nails, leaving a narrow space round the outer edge of the hoof. The cue widened from half an inch at the front to an inch or so at the rounded rear end, and there were four nail-holes at either side.

When taken to the smithy to be shod a farm boy and the blacksmith's apprentice had to be on hand, for the ox could not be taught to lift one foot at a time like a horse. The bullock was thrown down, usually on the grass patch outside the smithy, and the boys sat on its neck to keep it from struggling, while its four feet were tied to a tripod of iron poles. The nails were first greased by being pushed into a piece of pork fat. Shoeing the ox-team was one of the treats for the village children. Once on the ground, the beast submitted quietly; when it was over, and the children warned to get back, the ropes were untied and the assistants rolled off the massive neck (incidentally smelling strongly of ox and with greasy coats), then the great animal would rise slowly, almost majestically with no loss of dignity, shake itself and immediately commence to graze as if nothing had happened. When on rare occasions the animal resented the process or was pricked by a clumsy smith, then everyone present rushed to sit on the creature to keep it down while the smith finished the job.

On Cotswold as in Oxfordshire and Wiltshire oxen wore collars instead of yokes. The collar was u-shaped because of the horns and put on upside down, fastened with a strap and then twisted round until the buckle and strap were on top and the thickest part of the collar rested on the brisket or chest. The hames were often of wood (Pl. 170). Instead of bits to the bridles there was a chain under the jaws, as in the pictures in some old manuscripts, and a rein on the left side only. The name for this chain varies; I have heard it called the mullen or cropper. Like the rest of ox-trappings it became very greasy with wear, so greasy in fact that the spring lock fastening it would sometimes fall open on its own. The pad or saddle taking the traces was made of wood and looked like a hump on the back of the trace-ox, 'where the rutch-chain goes through to hold up the sharves', as Mr Smith, who was in charge of the oxen on Lord Bathurst's estate of Oakley Park, Cirencester, explained to me as we stood beside Captain, the trace-ox (Pl. 171). That was about 1937 but I have never forgotten Captain, with his curved, spreading horns, magnificent deep chest and short sturdy legs, standing there, patient and docile, awaiting the command to move as his harness was adjusted.

Mr James Farmer, who farmed Oxlease Farm near Filkins and who is now well into his nineties, told me that wooden hames were used on both oxen and horses on his father's farm but that the ox-hame had the 'draw-bar' higher, the draw-bar being his name for the trace attachment. The line of the pull was along the ox's backbone for the ox carried his neck flat, whereas a horse pushes with shoulder and hock. A horse, if he could not get a load moving by using his weight, would give up but an ox would move forward step by step and shift a heavier load than two horses. He told me how he remembered the thresher coming to Oxlease Farm. There were two horses to pull the engine, but the drum, which was heavier, was drawn by a bullock, although so slowly that at first he could hardly see it moving. A great deal of their bulk was muscle and when after a few years' work oxen were sold to the butcher the meat was lean and sinewy and not fat as one would expect. Another man told me that when they were obliged to shoot a bullock which had broken his leg, joints of meat from the carcase were given to the men and this was so tough they had to beat it with hammers before they could get their teeth into it. His wife boiled it all day and then it was not soft.

The leather part of the harness was always very pliable because of the greasy skin of the beasts, and this grease soon rotted the stitching so that the harness needed constant repair. Buckles and straps would come undone of their own accord and it was never difficult on an icy morning to harness the team for work because the leather was so supple, unlike the dry hard harness of the horses so difficult to manipulate with frozen fingers on a cold winter morning.

Mr Farmer said the oxen were cheap and easy to feed; poor hay and 'almost any old rough stuff', bulk rather than goodness was their ration. They were content with rough shelter, for they grew thick coats in winter, and a yard with an open-fronted shed sufficed, while the horses needed a watertight and windproof shelter if they were to be kept in good condition. None of the various people I have asked about oxen could remember any particular vices, if their slowness was accepted, and farm workers were willing to do this and appreciated it because it was allied to docile acceptance of work. The only times they were troublesome was when the flies were biting and then the whole team would kick up their heels and make off in a wild pounding gallop, upsetting waggon, load, or plough.

The last team of oxen to be worked on Cotswold and in England, was Lord Bathurst's, which survived until about 1945 as a working unit hauling timber or drawing harrows, though by this time they had ceased to be a necessary part of farming economy and had become a picturesque symbol of Old England to attract the crowds at local Fairs and Carnivals. They were paraded at the Royal Tournament at Olympia in 1932 and took part in several films, including *The White Ensign* in 1933, modern progress having turned the humblest of farm animals into film stars; but I have no doubt they took this translation with true bovine placidity.

# Horses

HORSES, unlike oxen, need considerable care and attention to keep them in good condition and the carter's work was more than harnessing, carting, ploughing, feeding and watering and putting them in the stables when the day's work was done. He usually had other men or a boy to help him but the responsibility was his. It was not a one-sided affair, the horses reciprocated, especially if they had been trained and worked by the same man for years, and one of the early objections to the tractor was that 'it wasn't pleased to see you in the morning like a horse'. The carter usually loved his horses, though he rarely confessed to it, and derived satisfaction from the understanding between them and himself. They served him and he served them, cleaning out their stables, not as with oxen a rough mucking out of their yard and rough shelter when there was time to spare, but as a serious regular job. A horse kept much fresher in a clean stable and most carters tried to make the stables draughtproof, even to not brushing down the cobwebs from the walls, it being a superstition that horses would catch cold if the cobwebs were swept away, but whether this was because cobwebs were thought to have mysterious properties I have never been able to discover. Most men did not question the old lore. On several occasions, though, I remember men who had cut themselves rushing into an outhouse to find a mass of cobwebs to put on the wound.

I never saw the teams of horses, as many as eight in a team, and eight or more teams to a field, ploughing the wide Cotswold fields but to those who did the memory still brings a gleam of pleasure. 'You should 'ave seen them', one old carter said to me as if he felt I had missed one of the seven wonders of Cotswold; and perhaps I had.

At one time a picture often hung on cottage walls, the original painted by a Victorian artist, showed such a scene, with a blue sky and white billowing clouds, orange-hued earth, the coloured horses and flocks of white gulls and black rooks following behind the plough, pictures given away by tradesmen or bought for a few pence at the fair; and it pleased the farm worker as belonging to his own way of life.

It was the pride of those who farmed in a big way to match their horses, it was the pride of the carters to turn them out sleek and glossy, with shining harness and polished brasses and with tinkling bells as well when they went on the roads drawing waggons of hay or corn. A man would work to the limit of his strength at harvest and still rise early enough to groom and polish and start each day with a well-turned-out team. The horses were more important than the men; they were also more expensive to keep and less expendable.

'Good horses, good farm', I have heard it said. When he went after a new job or to another farm for any reason the carter had sharp eyes for the horses and their stabling. If the horses looked well-fed and groomed then it followed the rest of the farm would be in good order.

Competition between the head carters on different farms went to extravagant lengths. Although among the better paid farm workers, their wages never went far beyond subsistence level, particularly if they had a large family, yet they would spend money on braid and brasses to decorate their teams on fair and feast days, and spend their meagre spare time decking them out to make a grand show.

Carters had a few extras as a result of their job, beer money when they went on night journeys with loaded waggons taking grain to the big mills at Tewkesbury, Cirencester and Gloucester, a larger piece of beef at Christmas. Horsehair, used for many years for making mattresses and furniture cushions, was another small source of income. Men travelled from farm to farm collecting it from carters who accumulated a little store from combings. A few men might tweak extra hairs from the tails of their horses but mostly they were too proud of their animals to do this. At one time carters had to be on the look-out for horsehair stealers who would strip a horse's tail in a few moments if the team was left unattended.

Carters had their own herbal remedies handed down like the brass ornaments and bells from father to son. They concocted the salves and potions themselves, either growing the plants in their gardens or seeking for them in the woods and fields. Bearsfoot, *Helleborus feotidus*, was for conditioning and was used extensively around Chipping Campden not only for horses but for sheep. It is still used today in this district for sheep and one finds it in many a neglected corner of old fashioned gardens, a relic of the days when a man believed in his own remedies. Walnut leaves were used for worms. One carter told me he used to walk several miles to gather walnut leaves which he dried and rubbed into powder before putting them into his horse's bait.

Before the horse ceased to be the chief means of haulage and ploughing, one way to see the various ways of plaiting and trimming horses' manes and tails was by visiting Stow Fair in May or October, where every kind of horse and pony was exhibited for sale, from the unbroken Welsh ponies who skittered about the streets showing the whites of their eyes, to the stolid great cart horses standing passive beside their masters, manes and tails braided and plaited, coats shining, their hoofs blacked. The carters themselves wore clean clothes, fresh kerchiefs and polished boots for the occasion. The colours of the braids were red, white and blue (for there was no man as patriotic as your old fashioned farm-worker), the braid eked out with yellow bass or straw. As much ingenuity went into the plaiting as went into the making of the corn dollies or 'Gloucestershire necks', indeed the same fingers usually made both, fingers toughened by years of work and often so rough one wonders at the delicacy of their handiwork.

The favourite pattern in the north Cotswolds was a close plait along the side of the mane and between the eyes, decked with bright yellow straw and coloured streamers, the tail bound into a club with close-trimmed tufts to finish, but the carter inherited various patterns from his father or grandfather and liked to use his own. I was once shown a 'Michaelmas' style for horses taken at Michaelmas to be sold. It was simpler than the plaiting for special occasions and was just a finish to the grooming. It was not a happy occasion for a carter to take his horses to be sold, 'and you hadn't much heart for the job'.

The most fruitful period for horse-brasses was from about 1851 to 1900. They came into use shortly after the Napoleonic Wars; before that time, although man had ornamented the trappings of his horses since prehistoric days, working animals had worn few trimmings other than an amulet or a few blue beads to keep off the evil eye. Brasses made between these dates can be recognized by the small studs used by the metal-worker to hold the castings in a vice while dressing and polishing the faces. Earlier ones were cut from metal entirely by hand and made by travelling tinkers who punched and pierced the pattern with home-made tools. Some of the finer examples were made to order by skilled metal-workers, and these were considerably more expensive. The brasses belonged to the carter or, in the case of small family farms, to the farmers themselves. Firms of carriers, brewers, posting houses also ordered brasses to their own desings. Gypsies had their own special brasses made by their own people and showing symbols having special meaning to the tribe; as many gypsies were metal-workers these became an expression of their skill.

The latten-bells, about the size of handbells, three or four to a horse, were fixed on the hames by a circular rod protected at the top and sides by a short leather curtain studded with small brass plates. A set of bells made the scale, and those I have heard, not on working horses but in private collections and museums, have a clear musical note and must have sounded delightful when the horses were trotting steadily. Their original use was to warn oncoming traffic in narrow winding lanes where it would be impossible for a waggon to turn, particularly at night. The small horse-bells were an ornamental device, an upright ornament sometimes finished off with a tuft of coloured hair like a shaving brush with the bells hanging below so that they tinkled whenever a horse shook his head (Pl. 164). Another head ornament was a 'swinger', a disc of brass which glittered as it swung to the motion of the horse's head.

The brasses themselves, plates or discs about three inches across, were fastened singly at the forehead (Pls 166–8), or several together on the martingale or breast-strap. Then there were brass studs, sometimes in the form of hearts, stars or crescents on the hame rein and others on the loin straps. The blinkers might have a small brass (Pl. 165) or the leather be embossed with a moulded design, a favourite one being cockle shells, probably originating in the cockle-shell emblem of the saint of travellers and pilgrims, St James of Compostella.

Words of command differed not only in districts but on farms in the same district. In times of unemployment men moved out of their own areas from neighbouring counties, and for other reasons as well, and kept their own calls, but some were general to a locality. On Cotswold to start 'Het' and 'Cup', a form of 'Come Up'; to turn to the right 'ge wish'; to turn to the left 'ge wier' and 'Come back 'ere', with the two syllables *ge* and *wit* occurring most frequently, though in the north the W is seldom sounded, a soft 'oo' taking its place. Most carters had their own words of command and with long association an accord was set up between driver and the leading horses, the reins as well as voice transmitting the driver's intention to the animals, and as the movements were the same day after day a good team would often anticipate their master's wishes. When fresh horses were introduced into a team they were put into positions where they were controlled by the more experienced animals until they learned the words or motions of command.

The stable had a corn bin, sometimes known as 'the ark', divided into partitions to hold bran and oats, and the carter had many tricks to get a little extra feed for his horses above the ration laid down by the farmer. A handful of oats above the ration put a gloss on their coats no amount of grooming could achieve and when there were several teams on a farm this could be expensive. Many are the tales told by retired carters of schemes to defeat a farmer's vigilance, schemes he would never have contrived to procure extra food for himself or his family. But horses seem to create this kind of devotion amongst those who work with them, and this devotion was returned. "ed work his heart out for me', one old man said, lamenting the loss of a favourite horse. 'He was a good 'un to go. When you went to fetch him for another long day's stint he'd greet you like you was his best friend and not going to work the guts out of him.'

## SADDLERS AND HARNESS-MAKERS

One of the jobs of the saddler's apprentice was to go round the farms and bring back harness for repair, and while a few carters were handy in mending their own and on a big estate a head groom had some skill for temporary repairs the majority of farmers depended on the local harness-makers. So great was the pride of some carters in the turn-out of their teams that they would often walk miles in their own time to the harness-maker to see the job well done.

The medieval saddler prepared and tanned the leather himself, but old records show this was frowned upon because of the unpleasant smell when his workshop was in a village street. By the end of the eighteenth century the saddler had begun to buy his materials from a tannery, the demand being too great for the small supply tanned by a local man. But although he bought his leather from a tannery he seasoned and oiled it himself.

Making the hemp thread used for sewing the leather was another job and was usually done in a pond well away from the village, again because of the unpleasant smell. Local hemp-retting, that is soaking in a pond to loosen the fibres so they could be drawn into threads, was started again during the last war, and care had to be taken that animals did not drink from the ponds or they would have been poisoned, though I should imagine that the smell alone would have repelled most animals. It certainly repelled most humans. One of the jobs of the apprentice to saddlery and harness-making was to prepare the thread needed for the next day's work by treating it with beeswax after selecting the different thicknesses for the various types of work, so that the thread would go smoothly through the tough leather. This was the last job before he put up the shutters for the day.

A tannery at Winchcombe worked by Thomas Hunt provided leather for the district in the late nineteenth century. His pits were at the bottom of Vineyard Street. According to Eleanor Adlard, Winchcombe's historian, a Mr Oakley remembered him going out in the morning to collect sheepskins from farmers and then carrying them home slung on a pole over his shoulder. A kind of bygone often forgotten by local historians is the variety of smells, some pleasant, some unpleasant, which enriched country life in those days. There was another tannery at the foot of Sudeley Street known as the Sexty Tannery, which was burnt down. Tanneries like other village industries often took over disused mills and the Sexty tannery was once a grist mill. The tanner's tools can be seen in the Winchcombe Museum and their names explain their purpose—sleekers, whiteners, flatteners, shaving knives, and waxing and finishing glasses.

# Sheep

FOR some 700 years or more Cotswold and sheep (Pls 178, 179) were synonymous. Even when the wolds became wide arable fields after the Enclosures, sheep were kept on the hills where they fed the land with their manure and compacted the light soil with their hoofs; the Golden Hoof as well as the Golden Fleece were Cotswold's assets in her golden age. Farmers of the old school believed no farm was complete without a flock of sheep and when sheep were folded on land later sown for corn the seed germinated more quickly, as if the bodies of the animals had warmed as well as fertilized it.

Correspondence between Offa and Charlemagne in the eighth century mentions woollen cloth from Mercia, and earlier, in the third century, cloaks woven from wool from Cotswold sheep were an article of commerce important enough to appear in a list of goods exported from Britain whose prices were fixed by an Edict of Diocletian.

The sheep came into greatest prominence in the Middle Ages when the district had its own breed, the Cotswold 'Lions', said to have been derived from sheep of a Flemish strain imported by Philippa of Hainault, or as some believe from a flock imported by Eleanor of Castille from Spain.

The Cotswold breed have been described in contemporary writings of topographers, agriculturalists and poets from the Elizabethans to the beginning of the twentieth century, and all mention the whiteness of the wool, the long necks, broad buttocks, and the lovelock over the forehead. The earliest come from Camden's *Britannia*; '. . . upon these hills are fed large flocks of sheep with the whitest wool having long necks and square bodies', and from Michael Drayton's *Polyolbion*:

> . . . *whose brows so woolly be*
> *As men in her fair sheep no emptiness should see.*
> *The staple deep and thick, through to the grain*
> *Most strongly keepest out the violentest rain.*
> *A body long and large, the buttocks equal broad*
> *As fit to undergo the full and weighty load.*

Marshall describes them as 'polled, long-woolled, middle-sized' but by this time, 1796, much cross-breeding had taken place, clothiers experimenting with new strains to produce a finer quality wool on a smaller animal that could supply mutton, the legs of the old breed being too big and fat for the palates of the nineteenth century.

A long and detailed description was written by Mr Swanwick of Cirencester in 1891. He was anxious to record the characteristics before they were forgotten, for by this time cross-breeding had greatly diminished the original flocks, though a prize flock was kept for many years by Mr Garne of Aldsworth where the greatest care was taken to keep the strain pure. 'Clear, fine, white faces, slightly Roman profiles, lovelocks of silk wool over the forehead, long, level and straight backs with slightly overhanging rumps, wide frame with well-sprung ribs, neck somewhat long and moderately thick, especially at the base and arching upward.' This long arching neck is to be seen on a sheep engraved on the memorial brass to Thomas Bushe, in Northleach church, a woolman and Merchant of the Staple who died in 1525.

Mr Swanwick also mentions 'the grand and noble bearing, full clean white legs', and ends his description with advice to breeders to aim at producing the greatest possible amount of wool upon a sheep 'so thoroughly adapted for carrying a heavy fleece'. Evidently he considered that the fleece 'open and curly and of considerable weight, sometimes in the case of hoggetts exceeding fourteen pounds' could be improved. There is no doubt he was an enthusiast for the breed.

As a result of crossing with Leicestershires the coarseness of the wool increased during the eighteenth century but it was in great demand for the worsteds for the East India Company, one of south Cotswold's biggest customers. One reason for the cross-breeding and the introduction of other breeds was the great demand for wool during the cloth trade booms. It was estimated that in 1757 there were 400,000 sheep on Cotswold and that Stroud alone needed some two or three million fleeces a year to fulfil orders for cloth, according to Dr Moir in her paper on the Gloucestershire Cloth Industry published by the Leicester University Press. As the more enterprising clothiers turned to Spain and then to Germany for wool of finer texture the wool from the old Cotswold sheep came to be used for stout heavy cloth for the Army and for the selvedges and tops and tails of finer cloths.

Although some Spanish merino wool had been imported into England before the cloth trade got under way it had made little impact generally until well into the eighteenth century, when a flock of sheep obtained from Spain by George III was put in the care of Sir Joseph Banks of the Royal Society. These sheep became very popular with sheep farmers and by 1802 Sir Joseph proclaimed that 'the demand for his Majesty's merino sheep had increased prodigiously, especially in Gloucestershire.'

Edward Sheppard, a gentleman clothier from Uley, whose blue cloth was as famous as the Stroud 'scarlets', crossed the merinos with his Ryelands, experimenting as he put it 'not under the idea of superseding the use of Spanish wool but to counteract the spirit of monopoly which prevails in the trade'. Playne's of Longford, another family of clothiers, introduced German wool in 1808, William Playne afterwards going annually into Germany to choose and buy the wool himself, until the German wool was superseded by the Australian wool, of which a factor wrote; 'There is a great kindness in the wool in the manufacture'. By this time the cloth trade had become too big to advance the old Cotswold breed of sheep and the sheepwalks were being turned into stonewalled arable fields growing barley, wheat and oats. Sheep had become part of the farming economy instead of being the principal crop.

The shepherds no longer followed their great flocks for miles across the open wolds but folded their sheep on the unploughed hillsides or on the stubble. The ploughing during the First World War of many hillsides once considered too steep, and the farming slumps of the 1930s reduced the flocks until sheep in any numbers on a Cotswold farm became a rarity. Today sheep-farming flourishes again on Cotswold with smaller, lighter breeds to suit the modern market; the old Cotswold lions have become living 'bygones' for the tourists. Some have been used for cross-breeding, the best known being the Colbred. Appropriately they are being reared on the wolds above Northleach where Will Midwinter and those other Cotswold woolmen who helped to build Northleach church once congregated to buy and sell wool in the fifteenth and sixteenth centuries.

## SHEEP-SHEARING

Before the Enclosures sheep-shearing time was as important as the corn harvest, more important probably to the great landowners who had turned their land into sheepwalks and derived much of their income from the sale of wool. From the twelfth century until the Enclosures many a cottager also kept a few sheep, the sale of wool giving them one of the few opportunities they had of making a little money. Some indeed by strict economy and long hours of work gradually increased their flock until they became small sheep-farmers themselves, and then went on to bigger things, lifting themselves out of the cottage class. Serfs by this means could find the money to buy their freedom when after the Black Death the lords of the manor commuted field services for cash.

June was the busy month, rounded off at the beginning of July with sheep-shearing feats and jollifications, and it was the time when not only the shearers were busy but the roads and tracks became alive with travellers, the Abbots and their stewards journeying from manor to manor to supervise the gathering of the fleeces, the merchants assembling in the little towns of Cirencester, Chipping Campden, Tetbury and Fairford, Northleach and others with their retinue of carriers and packhorses, and the King's men coming to gather in their dues on each tod sold.

Good weather was as important to sheep farmers then as it is today. A cold wet June meant a heavy loss, for wool packed wet loses its spring and quality, and the low temperatures after rain were dangerous to newly-shorn sheep. The Almighty does not always temper the wind to the shorn lamb on Cotswold.

Several shepherds have told me that a sheep's wool grows more quickly after it has been clipped by hand, perhaps because it is not shorn so closely as when a machine is used and perhaps because older men dislike any form of machinery, preferring their own dexterity, and criticize when they can. As at hay and corn harvest, as many men as can be spared on the farm help with the shearing, common effort giving rise to a good deal of chaffing, though not when the men are shearing for they must concentrate on the job; the shepherd sees to that. He is master of the proceedings and what he says goes. Shearing is sometimes undertaken by travelling gangs. You can always tell when it's shearing time, I was told, the men's hands through handling the greasy fleeces being 'as soft as a baby's bottom', or, as another man put it, 'as soft as a goose's breast'.

One of the shepherd's perks just before shearing is the sheep-dags, those matted ragged tufts of wool on the sheep's backsides soiled with dung and which are cut away before the sheep is shorn. This makes a splendid fertilizer for the garden, and is put in the bottom of trenches dug for runner beans and peas, and many a prize-winner in a local show owes his success to sheep-dags. The wool holds the moisture and the manure feeds the roots. I was once offered a bag of the odorous stuff and my pleasure at the gift made me a gardening friend for life. I discovered afterwards that Shep Boyes had been anxiously watching me to see how his gift would be received. It seems he had made the same offer to another woman in the village who professed to be a great gardener and she had refused it in disgust, whereupon she was taken off his list of people who might receive a special cutting or seedling, or a boiling of his giant runner beans.

Hand-shearers (Pl. 184) work on the principle of the sprung handle and in appearance differ hardly at all from those used in medieval times, except that they are now mass-produced and the metal, of course, is also produced by modern methods. There is a noticeable difference in the quality of the metal and general workmanship of the old shears; those bought in an ironmonger's shop within the last twenty-five years are inferior, even trumpery in comparison. A tiny pair of clippers identical in design was found in the excavation of one of the many Roman villas near Cirencester, evidently part of a lady's toilet set, so it would seem the principle was known in the days when Cirencester was Roman Corinium.

The bulk of sheep-shearing today is performed by machine, but shepherds still use the old-style clippers for the final trimming of sheep going to Shows. Where a farmer only keeps a small flock then they might be shorn by hand. But although obsolete for sheep-shearing, hand-shears are still part of a countryman's equipment and have a score of uses in the garden and on the allotment, such as hedge trimming and the cutting of grass verges. Many shears have been handed down from previous generations; like many other tools that have proved their worth they continue to be used by older people not so easily beguiled by the pictures of shining new implements advertised to do the job in half the time. Older countrymen are as conservative about tools as they are about their politics, they have learned the movements, they know how a well-tried tool will respond, they have an instinctive belief that old tools and old methods give the best results, and quickness is not all. Indeed, the longer it takes to do a job the better it will be done, in their opinion.

I once saw a thatcher neatening the edges of a thatched roof with shears. He had always used them for the job, he said, and kept sharp they did it well. His eyes twinkled as he went on to tell me that his father, also a thatcher, had cut his boys' hair with those same shears, finishing the job with scissors. On a Sunday morning or the morning of the day before a Feast or Fete day his father would cut the hair of his neighbours, a line of them waiting their turn to sit on the stool by the kitchen door. The 'rough' was taken off with the shears, the trimming was done with scissors. When all were finished the men would go off to the pub, where the barber was paid with free drinks, though sometimes a man would bring a block of wood, a few eggs, a bunch of spring onions and put them shyly on the kitchen table in payment. The clippings when swept up were put carefully in the middle of the rubbish heap. 'It was unlucky to burn them,' he said. When I asked why, he shook his head, 'Same as nail clippings.' His mother would never cut their nails on Friday or Sunday. 'They had a lot of funny ideas in them days', he said with a grin. But I noticed he always went round his ladder and not under it when he was working on the pile of straw below.

## THE SHEPHERD

The shepherd came top in the hierarchy of farm-workers subject to no man but the farmer himself, and a farmer with a good shepherd knew better than to insist too strongly on his own way. Other workers could be easily replaced, but not a

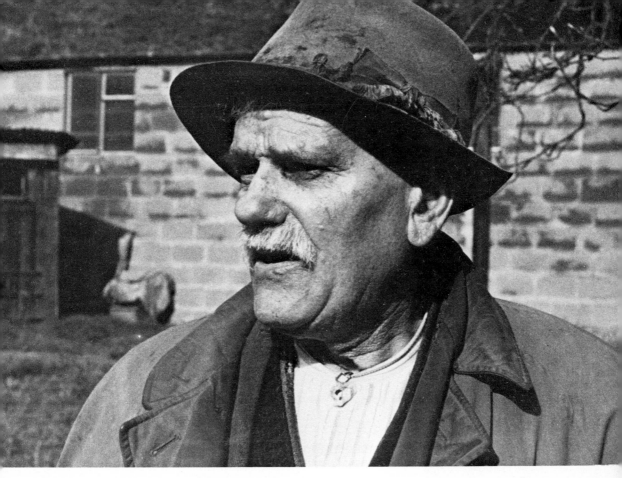

161. *Alfred Rastall, carter, of Ebrington.*

162. *Timber team, Winchcombe, in 1900.*

163. *Brass mount from noseband, from a set of harness made for the late Harry Steel, Home Farm, Selsley.*

164. *Plume and bells formerly belonging to the late Albyn Bingle, coal merchant, of Kings Stanley.*

165. *Blinker boss from harness owned by the late Fred King, Little Britain Farm, Woodchester.*

166. *Forelock brass with porcelain boss; formerly belonging to W. Knight & Co., Ebley Corn-mills.*

167. *Forelock brass of harness made for E. T. James.*

168. *Forelock brass owned by the late Arthur Pullin of Woodford Green Farm. Brasses can also be seen in Plates 137, 147.*

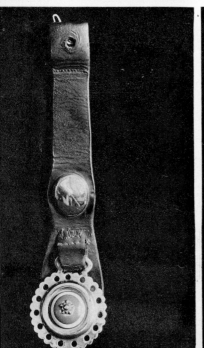

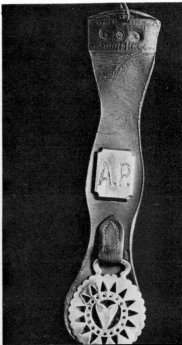

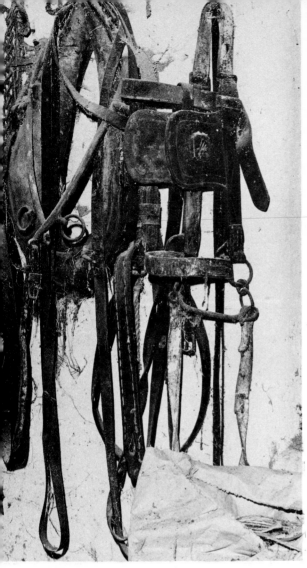

169. *Old harness, Little Britain Farm, Wood-chester.*

170. *Hames from ox harness, Priory Farm, Leonard Stanley.*

171. *Captain, the trace ox in Lord Bathurst's team.*

172. *Winchcombe market, 1905. From a photograph by J. P. Hawley.*

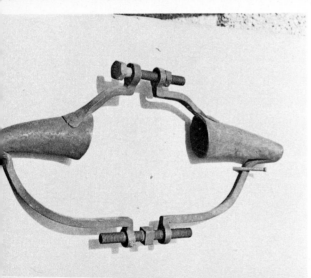

173. *Device, made by a blacksmith, for training the horns of show cattle. Collection of Mr R. Soule, Southrop.*

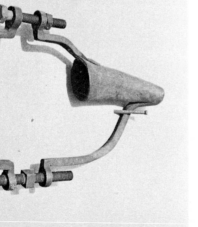

174. *Drenching-horn for cattle; Old Court Farm, Lower Stone.*

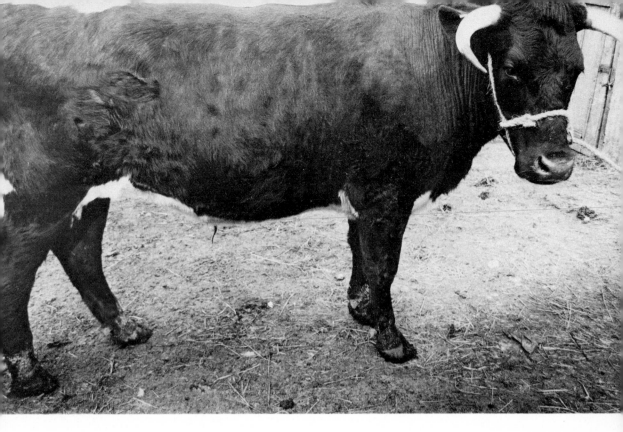

175. 'Egbert': Old Gloucester Steer.

176. Marking day,
Rodborough Common, 1971.

177. Rodborough marking iron.

178. *Shorn Cotswold sheep.*

180. *Bench-end in Stanton church, grooved by chains used to tether dogs brought to church by shepherds.*

179. *Cotswold ewe and lamb.*

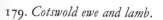

181. *Shepherd's smock; Northleach wool festival, 1970.*

183–185. *Crooks and shears from Kitesnest Farm, Whiteshill.*

182. *Crook for dipping sheep; Stowell Park.*

187. *Pig balance, Ebrington.*

186. *Shepherd's swede years old, used by Quenington.*

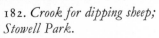

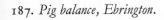

188. *Brawn press, used at Quenington.*

189. *Gloucester Old Spot weaner.*

190. *Gloucester Old Spot sow and litter.*

191. *Westington Quarry, Campden.*
*J. G. Strange and Sons.*

192. *Levering blocks.*

193. *The circular saw, Westington Quarry.*

194. *Mr J. Strange with chisel and mallet.*

195. *Work in the quarry.*

198. *Priest's door in the south wall, South Cerney Church.*

196. *Stone water troughs ('the Trows'), Frampton Mansell. The divisions are for washing and rinsing.*

199. *Churchyard steps, St Aedburga's Church, Broadway.*

197. *Large tiles used as fencing, with blacksmith-made metal ties. School Lane, South Cerney.*

200. *Stone stile, Barnsley Church.*

201. *Work of an unknown sculptor; roof-boss in South Cerney Church.*

203. *Exterior sculpture, Barnsley Church.*

204. *Capital in the chancel, Chedworth Church.*

202. *Late Norman font, Duntisbourne Abbots.*

205. *Carved detail on tomb, Minchinhampton.*

206. *Tomb of Valentine Strong, Fairford. It is inscribed: 'Here lies the body of Valentine Strong, Freemason who departed this life Dec 20 AD 1662'.*

shepherd who had proved his worth. He was the only one given his rank; head carters, ploughmen, stock men were known by their names but he was Shep, or Shepherd, a title of respect.

A shepherd's equipment has changed little down the years: the movable hut by the lambing pens is an improvement on the roughly thatched shelter of wattles and straw of medieval times, the oil stove or squat iron stove with a tin pipe through the roof an improvement on a charcoal brazier; the 'drove', a heavy pointed bar of iron for making holes in the ground for erecting hurdles; a wallet or old army knapsack for simple first aid remedies for his flock; the full-skirted khaki overcoat from Army surplus stores instead of the thick wide cloak to protect him from the icy winds that blow across the wolds in lambing time, though these old overcoats, relics of the First World War, are now giving way to anoraks and windcheaters.

Another part of a shepherd's equipment from the nineteenth century until the middle of the twentieth was his pipe, tobacco being a solace in his lonely job. An old shepherd, Walt Turner, once told me how he started smoking. I had met him leading his flock to a fresh hill pasture and as always stopped for a chat. He was excited this morning, his blue eyes brighter than ever. Most of the shepherds I have known have been blue-eyed.

'It's sixty years ago since I started smoking, sixty years today,' he said.

'You remember the very day?'

'It's my birthday, that's why,' he replied, puffing furiously. 'Can have a bit extra today, me granddarter gave me a new pipe and a tin of baccy.'

As he had hoped, for he loved to talk about the old days, I asked him about the birthday when he had first smoked. He had been twelve years old and his uncle, a shepherd, had got him a job with his own master as shepherd's boy. 'Shepherding was in the family. Me father was one, and Uncle Jobey and two cousins.'

The first thing Uncle Jobey did was to take the boy into the village pub and buy him half a pint of beer, a packet of tobacco, a clay pipe and matches. Then they went back to the sheepfold where his uncle showed him how to fill and light the pipe. 'He said I'd never make a shepherd if I didn't smoke and he wasn't having a boy otherwise, cos it was lonesome work, and a shepherd wanted summut. I was as sick as a dog and wished I was dead lying under the wall, but when it was time to go home I got up and Uncle told Mum I'd be better in the morning. She was proper scared, seeing me refusing me food. But I persevered because I wanted to be a shepherd like me father. I thought he was cruel at the time, he was a hard man, but there was sense in what he made me do for all that. He's been dead many a long year and he never made much out of shepherding. All he left me was his crook. Baccy and pipes was only a copper or two in them days,' he added wistfully.

Another time I remembered him saying there must be thousands of broken clay pipes where shepherds had minded their sheep, because they did not last long and one could get a clay pipe for nothing in some pubs. Years after, his words came to my mind at an excavation which had laid bare several acres about a hill-top. Under the turf were the broken bowls and stems of old clay pipes, some going back a hundred years or more. This must have been a favourite resting place of shepherds, I told myself.

Another item of Shep Turner's equipment was an old lantern, or lanthorn, for the windows were of horn, and though he was pleased with my interest in it he could not tell me how it came into his family's possession, only that it had hung on the same nail in the lean-to scullery of the cottage where he was born, and when his parents died he had taken it to use at lambing time. He was contemptuous of torches, 'batteries run out and where are ye', and the soft light of his lanthorn did not startle the sheep. I had the impression he considered it more fitting not to stab the night with shafts of brilliant illumination, that this made the wolds strange instead of the familiar place he knew so well. I regret now I never saw him at night with the old lanthorn held high so that he could see each ewe in her separate lambing pen, hurdled against the cold. Not that I could be sure he would have allowed me to do so. Visitors were unwelcome close to the lambing pens, and dogs forbidden. His own dogs were left at home except one old dog chained to a stake by his hut to warn him of intruders lest they frighten the ewes. Everything was done to keep them safe from all hazards. Shep received a small bonus for each lamb but the stronger incentive was his sense of responsibility to his animals and his job.

CROOKS

The Cotswold shepherd's crook (Pls 183, 185) follows no clear design, though it is generally said that the narrow part of the opening has to be wide enough for the shepherd's thumb to pass through and shepherds, according to the crooks I have examined, seem to have thumb joints larger than most men. But then, on the whole, they seem to have been tall men with big bones; perhaps the amount of walking they had to do from the days when they began as shepherd boys has something to do with this, or the fact that they were among the better paid farm workers and fed better in the days when sheep were allowed to roam more widely. Shep Mathers, a Wiltshire shepherd, came to the Cotswolds when his master sold his flock and ploughed the downs where they had fed. He had been a shepherd some forty years and had a remarkable succession of cross-bred collies, lean, rangy ragged-coated animals, and many a stew Shep and his family enjoyed made of rabbits and hares caught by his dogs. On one occasion his master caught him taking a hare from a dog's mouth but, as he put it without a smile, 'I told the gaffer I couldn't stop the poor creatures doing a bit of hunting. It was terrible dull for them looking after silly sheep and sometimes I let 'em go off for a run to break the monotony, like. I don't know if he believed me but a good shepherd's hard to come by and he was a poor payer so he gives me a warning and lets it go.'

Shep never ceased to lament the loss of his downs but he was enthusiastic about Cotswold hares. 'They told me they was as big as donkeys and I never believed 'em but the first one old Bet caught, well it beat any I'd seen back home. Lasted us nearly all week it did.'

A good crook lasted a shepherd a lifetime, and he often began his life as shepherd with one inherited from his father or other member of the family. They were made by local smiths, factory-made crooks not being a business proposition. They never wore out or rusted, the lanolin from the sheep's wool keeping the metal well-oiled, so that the demand was small. Localities had their own shapes but this seems to have depended more upon the smith than the shepherd. Like hand-made implements generally, the older ones usually have a better finish such as a delicately-curled end as if the smith enjoyed making that little extra flourish; those made towards the end of the nineteenth century rarely show these refinements and are finished with a flattened knob instead of a tapering spiral of iron.

## THE SHEPHERD'S SMOCK

The smock-frock lingered on until 1900. By this time it could be bought at a linen draper's or from a stall in the market, the material a cheap twill mixture of cotton and linen artificially stiffened so that after a few rigorous washings it became limp and thin, unlike the old coarse linen or drabbit which came up stiff as a board after each washing. The smocking was poor and meagre, being done by women in their own homes for a few pence a score, with the women buying their own thread. In the old days when the smocks were made by the shepherd's womenfolk they took pride in working rich and varied patterns and were more generous in the amount of material in body and sleeves (Pl. 181). They worked the long tight cuffs and wide collars with special designs to make certain the cuffs fitted tightly enough to keep the wrists warm, and shaped the collar so it could be pulled up about the neck and ears. They often made the cuff buttons, working spider web patterns on a linen base. There was a certain competition amongst young wives to turn out the best garment.

The shop-bought smocks came at a time when the pride in their handicraft had diminished, chiefly because times were hard and they had no time and no heart for such work. Many a woman who would have been proud to put days of work into a smock for her husband or sons had to take in the rough garments and sew for hours, often working into the night by candlelight to earn a few extra shillings which made all the difference to the household budget. One woman told me her mother rarely made more than half a crown a week but it was very welcome and meant they did not have to ask for parish relief. These smocks were sold at about five shillings each and this covered material, wages, overheads, everything but the thread for smocking. As a child she was sent to Moreton-in-Marsh to buy the thread, as it could be bought for a halfpenny cheaper there. Moreton was some three miles from their cottage and once, playing with some other children on the way home, she had lost the packet of thread and the memory of the anguish of having to tell her mother what had happened could still wring her heart.

'Mum didn't say a word when I told her. She just stood looking at me and then I began to cry and she put her arms about me and we cried together. I'll not forget it to my dying day. You see there wasn't another halfpenny in the house, and the man was coming for the work and with it not being finished meant no dinner until me Dad was paid his wages.'

The smock was a kind of overall garment, a round frock covering the body to just below the knees. The shepherd's smock was longer than those worn by other farm workers, to protect his legs in windy weather. If the other workers had long frocks they got too dirty in the dung and mud of the farmyard. The knees were also protected by straps or pieces of string tied just below them to keep out the draughts. The waist was protected in the same way in windy weather.

A good smock took about eight yards of material a yard wide. It was put on over the head. Fastenings let in the cold. It was warm once body heat had taken off the first chill, the average weight was about two and a half pounds. It was practically waterproof but once it became thoroughly soaked it was a cold and clammy garment where it touched bare flesh. In the shepherd's hut or kitchen there were always a smock and numerous jackets hung to dry in wet weather, a long depressing process making everything damp around them.

The colours were of natural unbleached linen, growing paler with each washing, occasionally blue for the north Cotswolds, perhaps because of nearness to Coventry, once renowned for its indigo dye; or a dingy olive green, the dye originally made from weld and woad locally grown, and afterwards from indigo and woad.

The cutting of a smock was simple. A double length of material about a yard wide was cut for front and back, and another length for the sleeves, each being half a width. Rectangular pieces made the collar, cuffs, shoulders and gussets. The main piece was folded and slit for the centre back and front as far as was necessary. The material was smocked before being gathered into the shoulders; the sleeves, after being smocked, were gathered into the shoulders, the cuffs sewn in and the side seams sewn up. Gussets gave freedom and extra width under the arms. The bottom part of the side seams was left open in a long frock to give extra freedom to the legs.

Smocking gave the garment elasticity as well as keeping it close to the body. The width of the linen was gathered, and to control the gathers rows of stitchery were applied, mostly a simple basket stitch. Depth of smocking was necessary to keep the smock in control, and the wavy chevrons, the scrolls, the feather stitching, the branching lines were folk patterns repeated the world over whenever women take up their needle and enjoy their work, instinctive patterns mostly made up by ringing the change on a few simple lines.

I do not think there is sufficient evidence to show that Cotswold smocks had any special design in style or ornamentation. Around the 1850s when smocks were general wear for farm workers the shepherd's wife usually reckoned to make a white smock for her husband for best wear, and into this she put every kind of embroidery stitch she knew, including feather stitching which had infiltrated from Wales, where it was one of the recognized forms of embroidery. Gloucestershire is near enough to Wales for this to have happened, moreover Welsh drovers in the eighteenth and nineteenth centuries were well known on Cotswold for it was on a through route from Wales to the markets of London. Cotswold was one of the drovers' resting places and there are several local spots known as Welshman's Corner, usually just off an old drove road, where the men used to camp for the night having put their cattle or sheep in a nearby field.

The smockers had no pattern books and learned from the older women, who had learned them from their elders in their time. The way of keeping the lines horizontal and the gathers vertical was to count the threads, easy enough in the coarse linen.

It would seem that the smock was being recognized as a form of English folk art by the middle of the nineteenth century and its making encouraged, for at the Great Exhibition of 1851 Esther Stimpson of Berkshire won a medal for her smock. When one looks at the smocks in local museums, and not so many have survived as one would have thought, it is noticeable that the women who worked the smocking and embroidery had the same sense of the balance of a design, the same homespun quality of putting a line in the right place, as the men who built in the Cotswold vernacular. They followed definite rules of proportion but within the limits of the convention their imagination had play.

SHEEP-BELLS

Sheep-bells went out of fashion after the First World War, when many thousands of acres of hill pasture were ploughed, the sheep enclosed in small fields or folded so that the shepherd no longer had to follow them as they ranged the wolds. The bells, made by the local blacksmith, belonged to the shepherd; he had them made, that is if he had not inherited them or acquired them from another shepherd, and they were prized. Some men even tried to match the notes so that the sounds were harmonious instead of a jangle. The bells were not circular like handbells but had flattened sides to fit snugly on the sheep's front and were hung on stout leather collars. These were fastened round the necks of the leaders and elders of the flock and the rest would follow where the bell-wethers led. The jingling of the bells told the shepherd in misty weather or if the flock had wandered out of sight in which direction they were heading. It is many years since I saw a flock with bell wethers but I still remember the air of importance, or so it seemed to me, worn by the belled sheep, though it was not easy to see the bells because they were hidden in the neck fleeces.

The sound carried great distances on the silent wolds and was one of those pleasant rural sounds now forgotten. The last bell I saw was hanging in a cherry tree in a large cottage garden near Chipping Campden some twenty-five years ago. It had lost its original clapper and several rusty nuts and bolts on a wire had been put in its place, and a length of rusty wire hung from it about the tree. It belonged to an old man who had lived in the cottage years ago. The cherry tree was known for its excellent fruit which he could sell at a good profit if the birds left him any to sell and he had rigged up the sheep-bell as a bird-scarer, attaching it to a long wire which went through his bedroom window so that he could tug it in the early morning and frighten the blackbirds. The local tale was that the birds awakened first and feasted at their leisure while the old man was sleeping off his heavy drinking of the night before. My interest in the bell prompted a neighbour to suggest I asked the blacksmith to find me one amongst the litter in his shed, but the blacksmith, routing about the sooty cobwebs on the wall, told me he was never asked for sheep-bells nowadays and since they were handy pieces of metal he had hammered out those he had and used the metal for other work.

# Cattle

UNDER the common field system with only one or two bulls serving the cows of the village and only sufficient fodder to keep the minimum number of animals alive from late autumn until the first bite of fresh grass in spring, the sixteenth- and seventeenth-century farmer stood little chance of improving his cattle. Scientific breeding as it is understood today had not been thought of and each region gradually evolved cattle best suited to the region. Cotswold had its Old Gloucesters (Pl. 175) derived from the red Glamorgan breed; as Gervaise Markham wrote in his *Cheape and Good Husbandry* in 1631, 'the red cow giveth the best milk'.

At the end of the next century Marshall records that the dairies of Gloucestershire had all been stocked with the old Red Gloucester cattle until in the middle of the eighteenth century the Longhorn, a North-country beast, had become more popular, proving suitable to the climate and other conditions of the wolds. The Longhorns kept their place for well over a hundred years and then experimental cross-breeding between Longhorns and Shorthorns, and between Shorthorns and Herefords, began. Shorthorns eventually replaced them.

The cows were not housed in winter on sheltered farms but fed with hay and kept in a pasture most convenient to the farm. On hill farms where fields were exposed to severe weather the cattle were kept in yards surrounded by open-fronted sheds.

According to a table compiled in 1970 for the Trust for the Survival of Rare Breeds only about a hundred females and four males survived of the Old Gloucester breed. One farmer today, Mr Peter King of Whiteshill, still keeps the old Gloucesters alive and his is the only commercial herd remaining in the county. The following description was supplied by him through Peter Turner, the photographer.

The Old Gloucester is a dual-purpose beast, fairly massive but notable for docility and longevity. Its milk approximates in quality to the Channel Island breeds, and its milk was of course the original source of double Gloucester cheese. A record at Sudeley Castle shows that in 1692 two beasts were received there for slaughter. The steers were widely used for draught purposes.

The Old Gloucester is slow to mature but reaches massive stature. The colour is dark mahogany with black or nearly-black face, legs and feet. A white patch spreading out from above the rump is carried on down over the belly, and the tail must be white. The horns are long, thick but pointed, and curve forward. A similar breed is widely used in Holland.

# Pigs: Gloucester Old Spots

THE origin of the Gloucester Old Spots (Pls 189, 190) is believed to be the West Country, particularly Gloucestershire, though it is difficult to say when or where they first became identified as a separate breed. Today more are to be found in Shropshire than in Gloucestershire. Like many of the old types of farm animals they are not altogether satisfactory for modern markets, though interest has revived in recent years due to the popularity of heavy pigs of 260–280 lb. liveweight.

Mr G. S. Cullimore, whose family has bred them for the last hundred years, describes them as very docile and hardy, good grassland pigs with the sows making excellent mothers, and this has been the general opinion throughout Gloucestershire for many years. Seventy years ago nearly all the pigs in the Berkeley Vale were Old Spots, and there have been many enthusiasts on Cotswolds in the past, including Colonel Dugdale of Sezincote, whose pig-man, George Radburn, used to declare they were more intelligent and easier to train than gun-dogs.

They are lop-eared, white in colour with black spots varying in size and shape, and they must have at least one spot to be registered. Mr Cullimore says that years ago they were darker in colour and no one has yet discovered the reason for the change.

# 4
# INDUSTRIES

*' . . . there's nowt tawdry here; all's solid.'*

# The Quarrs

THROUGHOUT history and prehistory there have been quarries on Cotswold. Neolithic man dug the stone to erect the chambered long barrows in which to inter the bones of his dead, the Roman-British built their town and country houses with stone they quarried on their estates, the medieval masons used it for monasteries, churches, tithe barns and manor houses and so on through the centuries until today. Quarrying has always been a way of life for a great number of Cotsallers. The evidence is plain on the ground. One cannot go far without seeing ancient quarries now overgrown with trees and shrubs, others with cliff-like faces and making caves in the hillside. Some are mere scrapes in the ground and others stone mines underground; one can see small pits in corners of fields near the gateway where a farmer has dug for stone to build walls and outhouses, and acres of 'gruffy ground' where stone for slates was taken from shallow diggings.

Today the quarries are even more evident for in the past two decades they have made great scars on the landscape where the ground is being eaten away by the jaws of huge mechanical diggers and grabbers after the stone has been loosened by explosives. The diggers deposit the stone in lorries and it is driven away to be mixed with cement and made into artificial stone bricks. These bricks can be laid more quickly and cheaply nowadays than stone by a mason using his traditional skills, and which came first—a shortage of masons or the invention of stone bricks —I have never discovered. The artificial stone brick has been the answer to cheaper building on Cotswold (Pl. 7) that will not spoil the harmony of the locality and those who dislike them receive some comfort from the fact that they are less out of place than red bricks would be.

In the days when quarrying was more than wholesale extraction of the stone from the ground a quarry began with an area roughly arc-shaped being cleared of topsoil and the first few feet of stone brash and poor quality stone lying just below the surface until solid rock was revealed. The first levels have their own names and differ from quarry to quarry, but usually follow the order of brash at the top in the subsoil, layers of clay, hard weatherstone and rag stone and then the best stone of all, the freestone used for carving and ashlar work. Weatherstone is fairly soft and soon scours after exposure to the weather, but a good freestone hardens on contact with the air and goes on hardening as the years go by. There may be a little crumbling of the surface at first but the heart of the stone remains sound, and indiscriminate cleaning and scouring does harm by revealing a new surface to crumble in the same manner in a few years.

As stone is quarried the original area extends, eating into the hillside until after a couple of hundred years a fine amphitheatre overhung by a cliff as high as fifty to sixty feet results. A cartway of easy gradient naturally evolves from the mouth as the sides gradually widen, leaving a broad level floor where the quarried stone can be stacked for measuring after being roughly dressed. This floor, because of the continual abrasive action of the stone being moved, becomes covered with fine stone dust, while larger fragments falling away beyond the level part make a scree where tiny limestone plants find roothold, clinging to the ground in close rosettes of leaves to keep life-giving moisture over their roots and bringing forth flowers bright as alpines in their season. Every field botanist knows what a happy hunting ground an old quarry can be for native limestone plants.

Stone in the old days was sold in yards, and could be seen in neatly squared lots, in all stages of age from hoary grey to the bright cream, yellow or buff of stone newly dug, the colours and qualities differing not only according to the district but to the uses of the stone. Stone for drystone walling, for instance, was kept apart from building stone, and in some quarries the banker masons and walling masons had their shed where the stone was dressed ready for the builder.

Various districts and various quarries were known for special qualities, such as Farmington near Northleach for its hardness and soft creamy colour, with rock of good quality going down two hundred feet or more. Taynton stone, known as far back as the Middle Ages for its quality of enduring fire, was used for malt kilns and ovens, and because of the large size of single blocks that could be taken out for 'troughs and Cisterns, and now of late Mesh-vats for Brewing . . . and one that held about 65 bushels drawn home with no less than one and twenty horses', to quote Dr Plot, Oxfordshire's historian, writing in 1701.

The Painswick stone is grey and gleams silver in the sunlight. One notices it on the clothiers' houses and their tombs in the churchyard, the stone despite its years of weathering keeping some of its pale tones amongst the dark avenues of yews. Catsbrain quarry near Painswick provided stone for Gloucester and Southwark cathedrals and the Criminal Courts of Old Bailey. Upton quarry, which once belonged to Christopher Kempster, has a pale creamy hue and is best for interior work because of its softness and the way its surface can be smoothed to a satin finish.

One can tell a district where there is good building stone under the ground by the excellence of its masonry. The villages along the Windrush, for example, beginning with its tributary the Sherborne Brook with Farmington at its source to where it leaves the hills as it comes to Witney, have been renowned for their stone since the Middle Ages. At the village of Windrush stone was mined until the beginning of this century, when the quarry was closed because new safety regulations made its working too expensive. Quarrymen who worked the mine said the beds were laid so true that little propping was needed, but for the safety of all quarry men the regulations were necessary, for not every stone mine was like the one at Windrush. Like most Cotswold quarries at that time it was worked by a family without large resources of capital and when the new regulations became law business was on the decline. It is interesting to notice that after the turn of the century the headstones in Windrush churchyard began to be made of blue lias, that cold smooth stone which never takes on the hoary bloom of oolite and its kindly accretions of lichen. These later memorials are in strong contrast with the older tombs and gravestones clustered around the church, which have a distinction all their own pointing to a fine tradition of local craftsmanship from the seventeenth century and dying out towards the middle of the nineteenth.

A mile or so east along the river the stone for the farmhouses and cottages of Great and Little Barrington came out of the famous Barrington quarries. At Little Barrington a half ring of cottages was built on the rim of a broad shallow bowl left when the stone had been taken from it.

The stone for the imposing Georgian baroque mansion of Barnsley Park came from the quarries on Quarry Hill belonging to the estate, a stone which has kept the crispness of its carving for well over two hundred years. John Price and Francis Smith of Warwick have both been named as its architect but whoever designed its imposing façade, the heavy pediments, the great Corinthian pilasters holding up the bold cornice, it would be the local quarrymen and masons who selected and dug the stone, who dressed the great blocks of ashlar and graduated their size and mortared the joints. The architect probably brought his own master masons to carve cornices and pilasters or to supervise the work but only the men who knew the quarry and its stone intimately could have selected its subtle variety of colour which has weathered to an even greater beauty and kept the outlines of the carving clear and decisive.

In the old days quarrymen knew the stone from their own quarries as a shepherd knew his sheep. They understood the way it could differ in strength and texture in different parts of the quarry, as well as the best way to get out the stone without spoiling the blocks. It came not only from direct experience but from the experience of the older men who had taught them their job. There was a tradition in Burford that masons coming back after working on the new St Paul's Cathedral in London had recognized local stone in the ruins of the old Gothic cathedral, and when I questioned if this could be possible Tim Rendle, who once worked a small quarry on an estate, assured me he believed it as he had once employed an old man who claimed to have seen Burford stone at St George's Chapel, Windsor, where he had been on a visit to see a nephew working there on repairs. To satisfy himself Rendle took the trouble to find out if this was possible and discovered that in 1474 a master mason called Jennings had bought stone from the Burford area.

This old quarryman had also told Rendle why masons were journeymen and had never been able to have settled jobs like other tradesmen but must wander about in search of work wherever there was new building going on. It seems that masons building Solomon's Temple went on strike and Solomon put a curse on them and said they would go wandering about the world for ever.

In early medieval times masons were often seized for forced labour when their rulers wanted a great building erected, and then when the work was done they would be turned off to seek new employment. The religious houses employed large numbers of masons and at the Dissolution these went off into the towns and villages seeking employment, so it would seem the traditional curse was still working. This has certainly been the lot of the mason since building began, except for those master masons who were quarry owners as well, and even those like the Kempsters and the Strongs found most of their work away from their home towns or villages.

Mr Rendle showed me how he extracted stone from his quarry. As he was only working in a small way and only when stone was required for repairs to the estate buildings, modern equipment would have been too expensive so he worked as his father and grandfather had worked before him. First he took me to the quarry face and examined it for joints. He wanted a block he could use for mullions and dressed stones around a new window being put in an old cottage. Working with a bar and a pick and assisted by another man, they slowly levered out a rough block, manoeuvring it until it stood upright with room for them to work. The two men then set to work swinging their scabbling axes until the stone was rough-dressed. They also made dents in the sides with a hammer and chisel so that the claws of the crane could get a good grip on it, for it was now ready to be put on a bank and sawn into lengths. The crane lifted the stone into the air and after what seemed a long time, so slowly and deliberately was each movement made, it was lowered on to the table. 'It looks easy but you can never be too careful. Men have been buried beneath blocks of stone before now,' Mr Rendle said. I remembered the apothecary whose bones with his purse and scissors were found buried beneath a monolith at Avebury when its great circle of stones was being restored to their original upright position by Alexander Keiller and his band of archaeologists. It was surmised that the apothecary had been helping to pull down and bury the stone after the Edict of Nantes in the sixteenth century had exhorted all good Catholics to get rid of the stones and so help get rid of a pagan belief in their magical properties. A little carelessness with the primitive tackle and he was buried under several tons of stone; as there could not be the slightest chance he had survived he was left there with the monolith as his gravestone.

The number of places called Quarry Banks, Quarry Hill, Quarry Field is legion on Cotswold, but without the name one knows that an area of humps and hollows overgrown by trees and shrubs marks a quarry now deserted. A quarry takes on the name of the man or family working it, and these have changed many times down the years, so it is not always easy to trace an original parish quarry. Campden's quarry, for instance, out of which the original town was built, has been known by various names. Today it is worked by Mr James Strange and his sons (Pls 191–5). One comes to the great spreading quarry face through a woodland path which descends into the floor of one of the old workings, and which now holds the workshops, the sheds, the engine house, a covered mouth of a shaft leading to the old stone mine no longer used. Beyond this floor the curving wall of another quarry still being worked towers above the buildings, a crane and tractor on its floor looking as small as toys in its broad expanse.

In a shed is a great circular saw with thin jets of water playing about the rim, the man in charge wearing a long black plastic apron and rubber boots, for this is a wettish job though there is a guard on the table where a block of stone is being sawn into lengths. A skilful man can work to a sixteenth of an inch but the cut must be a straight one. The man on the saw cuts about a half-inch into the stone and then leaves the banker mason to finish the job by hand; the first cut being made by the machine saves time on the job.

The tools need constant attention to keep them in good working order. It still surprises me as it did when I was a child to see a man sawing a piece of stone as if it were wood. This rarely happens now mechanical power can be produced with the flick of a switch but the skill must be there to control the power. One man I watched cutting lengths for mullions with a handsaw, a special job for a purist, told me hand sawing was easy enough, ignoring the sweat that was soaking the mass of dark curls on his forehead and the signs of easing of the strain when the cut was made. He took up a mallet and a tool he called a 'waster' and began to dress a piece of stone, finding it easier to talk when his hands were occupied. His saw, he said, had to be set several times a day, more often if the stone was very hard. Axes had to be steeled every three months. A tool could slip if it were not sharpened correctly, and a piece of stone be spoiled. When they were paid piece-work this meant a loss of money as well as pride.

Wandering around the rough scrub and woodland within the quarry area one could feel as well as see evidence of stone being dug here from the past 600 years, and I wished it were possible to unravel the years, to find the hollows of the first quarry and go through the centuries before coming at last to Mr Strange's electrically powered saw and the lengths waiting to be made up into the fireplaces which are his speciality, and which go all over the region and beyond.

Yet those men who worked the first quarries would recognize some, indeed most, of the tools being used today, the scabbling axe, the round wooden mallet, the wedges and crowbars and beetles, the hammers and the picks.

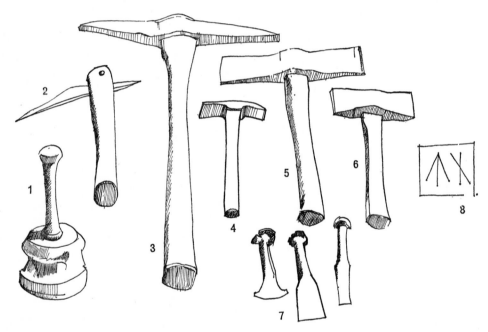

*MASONS' TOOLS, used by George Swinford*

*1, Mallet. 2, Slate pick. 3, Walling pick. 4, Slate hammer. 5, Walling axe. 6, Walling hammer. 7, Chisels. 8, Mason's mark.*

# Masons

THE greatest era of the Cotswold master masons lasted throughout the seventeenth until well into the eighteenth century. These were the days of the Strongs and the Kempsters, men who worked in the same way as the medieval quarry owners and mason contractors but because of the great need of their stone and their services after the Fire of London were able to increase their business and gain new and wide experience as they increased their fortunes. They were, in their fashion, architects as well as quarrymen, masons and sculptors; Sir Christopher Wren, Nicholas Stone and others might provide overall plans but it was left to the master masons to execute them, often with little supervision. We know from the accounts of St Paul's that William Kempster, son of the famous Christopher Kempster, was a master builder of considerable skill. Repair work carried out recently on the circular staircase at St Paul's, known as the 'floating staircase' because it had no central newel, revealed the mystery of the unsupported steps. The perfect rabbetting or joining of one step into the other sent the weight flowing down the well, and no man without a knowledge of stresses and strains could have built such a staircase. William was also called in when there was trouble in the crypt over the adjustment of the weight of the mass of St Paul's, and here again he solved the problem.

The rebuilding of the City of London gave them their opportunity because London possessed too few builders and lacked the materials when it was decreed that brick and stone must take the place of wood and wattle and daub; Londoners had discovered to their sorrow that wood and wattle burned too fiercely and too easily. Churches were to be rebuilt of stone, including the old Gothic cathedral of St Paul's. Eighty-nine churches were burnt and it was these churches with the new St Paul's that the Burford and Taynton masons helped to rebuild, not all of them with local stone but as much as could be quarried. It was transported in barges down the Windrush and the Thames to St Paul's Wharf in London, or put on great lumbering waggons and taken to Radcot Bridge on the Thames, as we know from Christopher Kempster's Day Book discovered in an attic in the loft of his house long after he was dead, the stone being from his own quarry at Upton near Burford. Thus from comparatively small beginnings the master masons of the Burford and Taynton area became mason contractors on a large scale.

We first hear of Timothy Strong, father and grandfather of the various Strongs who achieved renown for their work in London and Oxford, in 1617 when it is believed he leased quarries at Little Barrington and Taynton, a mile or so west of Burford on the Oxfordshire border, 'to serve the county with what was wanted in the way of trade' with the stone from his quarries, the masons, apprentices and labourers he employed.

The word 'county' is significant here, because by 1675 Thomas Strong, grandson of Timothy, signed his first contract with the Lords Commissioners and others for building a new cathedral of St Paul's, it being decided that it was impossible to patch up the old one after the Great Fire, though actually it took battering rams and gunpowder to clear away the ruins. Christopher Wren was chosen as architect, Thomas Strong became the principal contractor and laid the first stone of the foundations on the 21st June 1675, assisted by the Bishop of London. Thomas Strong wasted no time in starting to work. In the cathedral accounts of July 1675 his name appears in reference to work already done on the foundations of the Choir, from the centre of the apse to the centre of the East window of the south aisle.

Timothy Strong built the south front of Cornbury Park, Charlbury, for the Earl of Danby between 1630 and 1632 to the designs of Nicholas Stone, and 300 or more years later men from Burford doing restoration work found the mason's marks of Timothy's men on the old stones.

Valentine, Timothy's only son, rebuilt several houses in the Cotswolds including one for John Dutton, a Sherborne wool merchant, and he was at work on a house at Fairford in 1661 when he died. He is buried in Fairford churchyard near the south porch under a table tomb (Pl. 206). A Purbeck marble panel let into the side gives his name, the date of his death and the word 'Freemason'. A second panel now lost bore these words:

> *Here's one that was an able workman long*
> *Who divers houses built, both Fair and Strong.*
> *Though Strong he was, a Stronger came than he*
> *And robbed him of his life and fame, we see*
> *Moving an old house a new one for to rear*
> *Death met him by the way, and laid him here.*

Valentine had six sons, of whom Thomas and Edward worked on St Paul's, Edward to the end. Valentine seems to have spent his life in Taynton probably in charge of the quarries; Timothy and John, both masons, moved into Berkshire. John had a large family and there were Strongs living in Stanford in the Vale, Berkshire, as late as 1866, according to Lt-Col. R. Mills of Barrington Grove, the historian of the Strong family, and some of the finest tombstones in the churchyard there are by the Strongs.

Thomas took over his father's business and when masons outside London, under emergency regulations, were allowed to take up their freedom Thomas secured the Freedom of the City and membership of the Masons' Company in 1670 and was thus allowed to contract for three churches including St Stephen's, Walbrook, under Christopher Wren. It was at this time that he began to work with Christopher Kempster. The accounts for St Paul's for April 1678 record that he had thirty-five masons working for him at this time, but he did not live to see the cathedral completed. There is no doubt that he was one of the outstanding builders of his time. He was buried in Taynton in 1681, leaving his business to his younger brother Edward. In his will he directed that a legacy left to his sister Lucy should revert at her death to his executor, the money to be spent 'to make a way between Barrington bridges in Gloucestershire, so that two men may goe a front to carry a corpse in safetie'. In making this bequest he was following an old custom of merchants and others in medieval times when the repairing of roads and bridges was a pious act. On the bordure of the memorial brass of Thomas Fortey in Northleach church, 'a worthy merchant upright true and kindly', interspersed with tiny stops representing animals and birds, we read that his pious work was the repairing of roads and bridges. Thomas Strong's causeway to make the going over marshy ground less hazardous in bad weather is known as Strong's Causeway to this day.

Edward Stong continued his brother's work in London, increasing the family business not only by the important buildings he worked on there but by selling Barrington and Taynton stone from his quarries. He became an authority on Portland stone, realizing that the rebuilding of London churches with stone from the Burford area was not possible.

The accounts of St Paul's for 1698 show that Edward Strong had forty-four stonecarvers, masons and apprentices, while Kempster with his partner Beauchamp employed twenty-five. It is probable that many of these were Cotswold men who had accompanied Strong and Kempster to London, for a master mason preferred men who knew the stone they were working and who had probably helped quarry it.

We know a good deal about the Strong family because Edward, when he retired at sixty-two and went to live at Hide Manor in Hertfordshire as a country gentleman, having amassed a fortune enabling him to do this, wrote his *Memorandums of*

*Several Works in Masonry done by our Family*. He left these words to be inscribed on his tombstone:

'In erecting the edifice of St Paul's several years were spent, from its foundations to his laying the last stone and herein (equally with its ingenious architect Sir Christopher Wren and its truly-pious Diocesan Bishop Compton) he shared the felicity of seeing both the beginning and finishing of that stupendous fabric.'

The delicate way he associates himself with Sir Christopher Wren and Bishop Compton is an indication of the status he had acquired.

As far as we know Christopher Kempster never wrote his memoirs; he was a man who preferred working with stone rather than a pen and who had no desire to be a country gentleman of leisure. Despite the great contribution he and his son William made to the building of St Paul's, at least a quarter of the fabric, he remained a Burford mason and quarryman to the end. He built himself a house near his quarries at Upton and carved over a window CHRISTOPHER KEMPSTER BUILT THIS IN 1698, but he did not retire and live in it permanently until 1707 when he was eighty years old. This is the last date his name appears in the St Paul's accounts, where it is stated that the Dome was finished. By this time he must have felt he could return to Burford for a well-earned retirement. He was buried in Burford church some eight years later and his son William carved a cherub's head in white marble and put it above the stone of the floor covering his father's body. A quotation from a letter written by Christopher Wren to Bishop Fell concerning the building of Tom Tower, Oxford, recommending Kempster, could serve as his epitaph: ' . . . a very able man, modest, honest and treatable . . . he is very careful to work trew to his designs and strong bonded work and I can rely upon him.'

These are the men the world knows about, but what of the thousands of other masons and quarrymen who built the fine wool churches, the manor houses, the barns and farmhouses, the cottages and cattle sheds? Every town and parish had its quarry and it seems likely that before the Enclosures it was not difficult for anyone who wanted stone for building, if he was prepared to dig for it, to obtain it for nothing. After the Enclosures the stone pits and quarries became the property of the people owning the land on which they were situated and were leased to builders and masons. We know this happened, for instance, in the Campden area, when the parish quarry on Westington Hill on land belonging to the lord of Campden manor was let to Thomas Woodward, mason, on 5th September 1719, fine, £10, rent £3, for lives of lessee, wife Mary and son.

Thomas Woodward and his son Edward did a considerable amount of building in Chipping Campden and neighbourhood. Thomas took down Blockley church tower in 1724 and built the tower which now stands at the cost of £500, which, even allowing for the value of money in those days, seems a modest return for erecting such a large and dominating structure, though some of the stone used came from the old tower. Thomas copied the medieval outline and gothic bell-openings and hood-moulds from the fifteenth-century Campden church, but by this date the Perpendicular style had had its day and bold and upstanding though it is, Blockley church tower lacks the grace and fine proportions of Campden tower.

Thomas Woodward was happier with Bedfont House in Campden High Street, built for the Cotterill family, a fine eighteenth-century house of two storeys raised on a basement, with a central doorway reached by a flight of steps. The façade has two bays divided by fluted Corinthian pillars and a deep cornice with a balustraded parapet. One feels that Thomas and his son Edward were happier with the new fashion and it is believed that most of the classical ornament and façades in Campden were their work. The Woodward tomb shows their partiality for the Classical Revival, for its table top is carved with inverted flutings and surmounted by an inscribed urn, and records the death of Thomas in 1748, aged seventy-six, and of Edward, his son and partner, who built the tomb, and died in 1766.

An earlier stonemason, William Atkins, has a mural monument with a Latin inscription in the north aisle of Campden church but I have not been able to identify any work done by him, though families of that name are to be found in Campden records listed as freeholders from the beginning of the eighteenth century until the end of the nineteenth. A Jas. Atkins, who may not have any connection with the family, is described by Campden's historian Rushen as a 'little consequential man' and was nicknamed by the Campdonians 'The Royal Grig'. One of the amusements of the Campdonians was composing ill-natured doggerel about fellow townsfolk, for Jonathan Hulls, an early inventor of a steamboat, was also treated in this way.

> *The Royal Grig*
> *He bought a pig,*
> *He could not pay the purchase,*
> *He sold it to the Miller Keen*
> *Who sent it to the workus.*

Miller Keen at that time was a workhouse overseer.

## BANKER MASONS

Banker masons served an apprenticeship and were responsible for the carving of mouldings, ornament, cornices and the dressed stones surrounding doors and windows. Each had his own mark, which he incised on his work, a simple arrangement of a few lines less than an inch high. They were used to calculate a man's earnings, so many feet of cornice for example, and to show who was responsible for important and tricky parts such as joins where bad workmanship could ruin a whole section of the work. One of the earliest known on Cotswold is a T-shaped mark on the west wall of the south aisle in Northleach church, said to be of Norman origin, and others can be seen in Northleach church on the pillars, formed of a curious rhomboid with ends finished with crosses.

Banker masons were so called because they worked at a bank or stone bench. In a freestone quarry they worked in banker shops, that is rough sheds with open doors to give them a little protection from the weather. Banks were made by erecting a large flattish stone on piers of smaller stones, though when a man was doing a delicate piece of carving he covered the stone top with sacks to take some of the vibration of his tool.

Most banker masons have special tools made by the local smith to their own design as well as the usual equipment of scabbling axe, hammers—one called a 'kebble' for removing lumps from a knobby piece of stone—a 'chad' or 'jad', a form of adze. They used saws for stone cutting such as the stone ridges for roofs and mouldings, though today this work is usually done with a mechanical saw. Mallets were usually made of elm but one I was shown at Westington Quarry was of apple wood, worn out of shape by long use. The elderly man who owned it explained how he had made it himself, first using a compass to draw a circle, then gouging out the head with a carpenter's gouge and smoothing the whole with a rasp. He also explained that there were only two beats to a mallet, by right, 'it should be hit only on the beat.' An implement known to carpenters as a bevel was used for the angles of bay windows and when working in stone a bevel becomes not a bevel but a mason's shift-stock. Tools, such as chisels of every kind, used for the fine dressing of stone are struck with the mallet or hammer according to the shape of their head. There are also many kinds of drags in a banker mason's tool-kit, from coarse to the very fine used for smoothing away the marks of other tools. Talking to any banker mason one soon understands why they need such an assortment of tools, and how attached they get to a particular one as to an old friend. One man I knew refused to use a carborundum rubber, preferring to finish off with a piece of hard stone. He handed it to me.

'That's not Cotswold,' I said, looking at its gritty surface.

He grinned. He had hoped to catch me out. 'It's York stone and I use it with fine sand and water and it makes a finish like silk. A natural finish, stone to stone.'

The tools need constant attention to keep them in good working trim. In the old days a quarry owner often kept one man whose job it was to look after the tools and machinery, but most workmen preferred to look after their own, and generally put their mark on the handles so that they could always identify them. When a man died or was no longer able to work he gave his tools to his son, or left them to a special friend who he knew would appreciate them. A country auctioneer once told me he was often bid more for old tools than the cost of new ones, because men believed that an old tool had already proved itself.

# Stone Slates

THE climax of all good vernacular building is a roof of stone slates (Pls 212–14). Darker in tone than the walls because of their greater exposure to weather, the 'slats' keep the subtle variation of colour natural to the stone, the flaked edges and surface made by the slatter's hammer adding to the variation of texture. The use of stone slates during the Roman occupation was widespread, and Cotswold was rich in Romano-British country villas and town houses. Evidence that they were used between the withdrawal of the Romans and the increase in building of the early Middle Ages is not so clear, but we do know they were produced in the Guiting and Eyford areas in the twelfth and thirteenth centuries, showing that stone slates from these places were one of the sources of income of the Knights Templar who owned much land around Temple Guiting. Until a few years ago the ground around Kineton Thorns showed how these 'tile-pits' continued to be exploited through the centuries, from the oldest pits covered with ancient thorns and a thick mat of native vegetation which had taken centuries to cover the scars made by the earliest excavations to the diggings of the early twentieth century, when slates ceased to be dug in any quantity.

The Romano-British slates found on sites of Roman villas are roughly hexagonal, that is with the tail squared, but the general shape has changed little, being a rectangle narrowing at one end rather like a luggage label. They were fastened on the battens with an iron nail, and this is the way they are hung today, though in medieval times when iron nails were expensive wooden pegs were substituted for less important buildings. The pegs were made by chopping lengths of riven oak into sticks twice the length required, whittling each end, and then chopping it again to make two pegs.

In some districts the slates were bedded on moss, a long hair-like species which grows on marshy ground, but hay or straw was often substituted. In some instances when ancient slates have been stripped from an old roof there has been no sign of bedding material, though it may have decayed into dust. Mossing, or mosseying, was a special trade in the towns; in a village a mason could be slatter as well as

*Arrangement of slates up to the roof-ridge.*

builder and probably did the mosseying as well. In addition to providing the bedding for new roofs it was also the moss-man's job to renew it when it decayed. Owing to the steep pitch of stone-slated roofs rainwater runs off quickly but snow hangs on, and as the slates are porous the wet gradually soaks through unless the bedding prevents it.

In the earliest pictures of churches and cathedrals, mainly in illuminated books and manuscripts, buildings are often depicted showing roofs of wooden shingles and it has been inferred from this that the stone slate evolved from the shingle in an attempt to make a more permanent roofing material. But timber has never been plentiful on Cotswold and as stone slates were used during the Roman occupation it seems likely they continued to be used for buildings of any consequence in the centuries that followed. Tyley Bottom, near Wotton under Edge, could have received its name from tile pits long disused and now overgrown by trees. E. S. Lindley in his history of Wotton under Edge suggests that stone slates continued to be used after the Romans left Britain, contrary to the general belief that for several succeeding centuries no big buildings were raised, offering as evidence part of a Saxon Charter defining the bounds of a settlement in Wudetun which reads in Grundy's translation: 'First from the Ashtree along the top of the Ridge Slope to the Lea where tiles are made'. Grundy dates the Charter at about A.D. 940 but believed it to be a copy of an earlier document.

Not all slates came from special slate quarries. Most villages had their own quarries for building stone and in many cases tile pits near by, or stone suitable for roofing was obtained from the same quarry. Long Ground Quarry at Filkins, for example, because of the nature of its stone provides both building stone and stone for slates, for it comes in thin layers and advantage has been taken of this to provide not only roofing slates but thin rectangular slabs of stone called 'planks', looking like smallish gravestones, used for fencing, the planks held together by iron clamps made by the local smith (Pl. 197). Filkins has a famous slatter and mason, George Swinford, now many years retired. It was on an outhouse of his cottage at Filkins I saw some of the longest roofing slates I have ever seen, and his Museum of local bygones and many of the village gardens are bounded by planks taken from the local quarry. When Stafford Cripps, who lived at Filkins, opened up his quarry to provide new slated roofs for the village, George Swinford came out of his retirement and took on the job, and the village, now weathered and mellowed, has become an example of how a Cotswold village should be preserved.

Stonesfield quarries, renowned for slates, were opened at the end of the sixteenth century, and it was here, the experts say, that the frosting process was first discovered, that is the method of leaving the stone exposed during the winter so that the moisture in the thin films of clay between the layers freezes, thus expanding the pendle, as it is called, so that it splits easily into slates. In medieval and earlier times quarries were chosen where the stone split naturally, having been laid down in thin layers, and all the slatter had to do was to shape and trim his material. The stone at Stonesfield was mined, with shafts going down 60 to 65 feet and it was still possible to descend to these levels in 1859.

Quarrying began at Michaelmas and ended at Christmas. The men descended the shaft by climbing down a rope by which the stone was hauled up. The rope was worked by a windlass turned by hand or by a horse, depending on the level they were quarrying. The levels were only three to five feet high and the men had to crawl along and work in a stooping position for much of the time. When the pendle reached the surface it was wetted and covered with earth, the heaps looking rather like root clamps. This kept the quarry sap in the stone until the frost came. The ideal condition was a week's hard frost in January and this meant well-split slates and enough work to keep the men busy until the following Michaelmas when they would go again to quarry more pendle. Nature did not always produce the right conditions and in a mild winter any frost, if only for a few hours, was important. All the village would turn out to uncover the stone and spread it out. When frost occurred at night the church bell was rung to bring the people from their beds to uncover the pendle as quickly as possible. They did not curse having to turn out in the icy night air, for it meant work for everyone and regular wages for months to come. A mild winter meant disaster for the slatters and their families and they must shift as best they could until Michaelmas came round again.

The pendle in the clamps had to be kept moist throughout the spring and summer if no frost made it impossible to work, and this was done by growing a mat of greenstuff over it to keep in the damp. Once it dried out no amount of watering would restore the fissile quality to the rock. Even if left in a pond all summer it would not split when taken out: the stone was 'bound', and bound it remained for ever.

But if the frost came and all went well the slatters erected their little shelters of straw-covered hurdles or built themselves cave-like shelters of stone. Sitting on a sack or straw pad with a crapping stone between his knees, the slatter was all set to begin. The crapping stone was a narrow stone set edgewise upon the ground and on this he trimmed three sides of each slate with a special 'slat' hammer until it became the right shape and thickness. The final trimming of the edges was done by battering along them with the side of the hammer-head. The peg-hole was made in the narrow end by light taps with the point of the slat pick, the taps being directed towards the centre and the hole finished by knocking out the piece at the back without turning the slate over. Experienced slatters could perform these operations at considerable speed.

Mr Swinford explained how he found the spot to make the peg-hole by exploring the slate with his finger until he found a thin place and then, taking his pick, he tapped a small hole and bored it a little larger by carefully turning the end of the head of his pick round it. He always kept a dozen heads for his slat pick because they broke easily. For the heads he used old steel files, taking them to the blacksmith's to be shaped and sharpened. As he finished each slate it was put in a pile, 'ten flat and then ten edgeways, 250 was a good day's work.' His equipment was two slat hammers, a slat pick and some spare heads and a measuring rod. He found steel hammers not springy enough to give the right kind of blow, for the way the hammer reacted to the stone was very important. 'The smith splits the end of the iron and puts in a special piece of steel, while it's hot.' The hammers weigh about $2\frac{1}{2}$ lb; one he used with a cutting action, the other for battering the edges. The slat rule, or 'wippet stick', usually home-made, is marked with thin lines both straight and slanting and has a protruding nail at the top. The vertical strokes are used for sorting out the different sizes of slates. The nail is put into the hole of the slate and the length of the slate from the hole to the bottom gives its size and consequently its position on the roof. The slanting marks are to show the thickness of the slates, for the best work half an inch, for roofs of large expanse such as barns three-quarters of an inch. There were twenty-seven slanting notches on George Swinford's rule, all of them with names, though today slatters mostly use numbers.

His names, beginning with the roof ridge, were cocks, short, middle and long; short cutting, long cutting; muffett; short, middle and long beck; short and long bachelor; short and long nine; short and long wivot; short and long eleven; short and long twelve; short and long thirteen; short and long fourteen; short and long fifteen; short and long sixteen.

The other side of the rule is marked to give the battens the right bond—the battens being put on to suit the length of the slates.

The names and some of the sizes of the slates differ in different parts of Cotswold. A slatter who once worked in the quarries beside Buckle Street near Broadway gave the names as short and long pricks; short and long cutting; movides; short becks; short and long bachelor; short and long nines; short wivutts—probably the Oxfordshire wivot; and then continuing in long and short numbers to long sixteens. Another name for the row under the eaves was cussoms, or top-eaves, the next row being the followers. Duchesses and countesses are still remembered today, for I was once given these names by a young slatter who had them from his grandfather who taught him the trade. A seventeenth-century writer, Randle Holme,

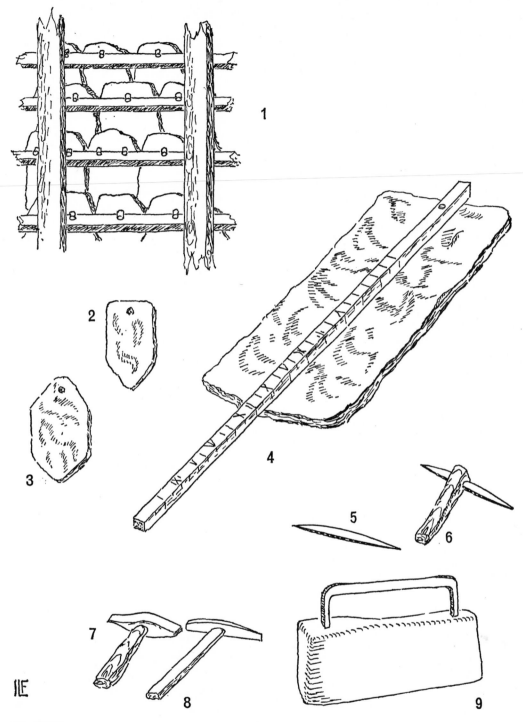

## SLATES

*1, Fixing on battens. 2, 3, Roman slates. 4, Slate on 'wippet stick', or slatter's rule. 5–8, Slatter's tools. 9, Crapping stone.*

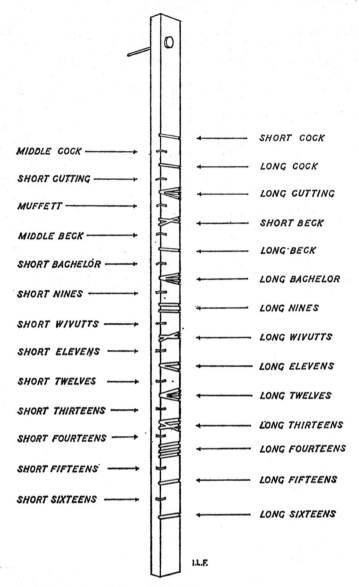

*'Wippet stick', or slatter's rule, from Moreton-in-Marsh.*

gives wivetts and bachelors but his farwells, chilts and warnetts have vanished from the slatter's vocabulary, or perhaps were never used on Cotswold. Rudge gives most of these names, with wippets and muffetty, which could be the wivetts of the north Cotswolds and the muffetts of Oxfordshire.

A slatter was judged by his swept valleys, always a weak part of a stone-tiled

207. *Waller, with stone axe, Hampnett.*

208. *Mr E. Pearce building a drystone wall.*

209. *Putting on the 'toppers'.*

212. *Roofing, showing graduated slates.*

213. *Slates sorted ready for roofing.*

214. *Scaffolding for ascending roof-pitch; Mr Gilbert Peachey, Chedworth.*

215. *Slatter's dressing-iron; Mr Gilbert Peachey.*

216. *Workshop of Mr A. Twinning, hurdle-maker, Quenington.*

217. *Fodder racks made by Mr Twinning, awaiting repair.*

218. *Mr Twinning with a hurdle.*

219. *Using a drawing knife at his 'brake'.*

220. *Hurdle-maker's tools: pick; frommard (cleaver); brace and bits; nails; mortise chisel; old horseshoe nails for 'stubbing' ends of stakes; drawing-knife; hammer; axe.*

221. *Hurdles made in Stowell Park estate workshop.*

222. *Wooden gate-latch, Cotswold style, Ebrington-Paxford road.*    223. *Gate-latch, Stowell Park.*

224. *A modern farm gate, Hampnett.*

225. *Hand-made plane for round chair-staves; Mr W. Gardner, Stow-on-Wold.*

226. *Hand-made cramp plane; Mr W. Gardner.*

227. *Thatcher's tools, used by Mr R. Soule and his father. Left to right: kneepad and rake; needles for house thatching; needles for rick thatching; spick hammers; sickle; spray-billhook; bond-twister, string-holders; barge-knife; double-handed barge-knife; hammer for barge-irons; two frommards; sheep shears in sheath. These tools belonged to Squire John Faulkner of Dunfield and when he retired the men were given their tools; these were given to Mr H. Soule.*

228. *Bee-skep with Cotswold stone base as landing board. Mr Fred Saunders, Sherborne.*

229. *Spring at Compton Abdale. Water powered the Cotswold industries of the eighteenth and nineteenth centuries.*

230. *Silk mills at Blockley, now converted to dwellings.*

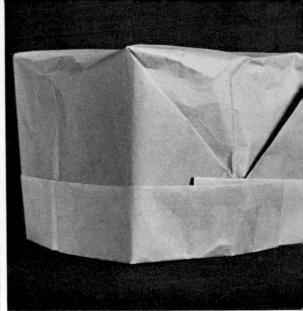

231. *Remains of a paper mill at Little Barrington.*

232. *Paper-maker's hat, worn in Postlip Mills, Winchcombe; made from 'deep tub-sized blue sampling' and regarded by the men as a valued symbol of their craft.*

233. *Paper Mill Cottages, Little Barrington.*

234. *Entertainment Committee, Ebrington, 1903.*

235. *Village band, Ebrington, 1903.*

236. *Club Day, Ebrington, 1900.*

237. *Mother's Union, Ebrington, 1900.*

238. *Club Day procession, Ebrington, about 1900. The two smaller banners represent the chief landowners of the village.*

239. *Country dancers, Stretton-on-Fosse, in the early 1900s. The servants of the Big House and villagers make the team.*

241. *Well-dressing parade, Bisley, 1971.*

242. *Bisley Wells, 1971.*

240. *Village feast, Stretton-on-Fosse, in the early 1900s.*

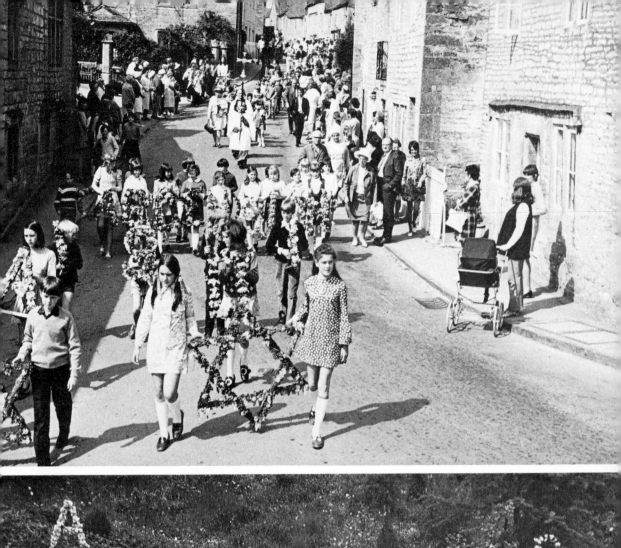

243. *Banner of 1856 carried on Club Day at Ebrington.*

roof. To bring the slates round in a sweep with a good overlap he must cut his 'valley stones' to a triangular shape and arrange them one over the other so that they left no cracks where the water could enter. This is sometimes called 'galetting'. Modern tilers sometimes use lead, but the old craftsman scorned such an easy method which was not only expensive but gave him no opportunity to use his special skill.

The ridge of a roof is often finished off with a sawn stone topping, rather like a miniature roof in itself, but before this is put on, or if no ridge is used, the third course covers the nail of the first course and this is followed throughout as, in three courses, the third just covers the nail hole of the first.

It is generally assumed that old roofs with concave curves from ridge to eaves have sagged because the rafters have sunk under the weight of the slats, but in some instances this is not so; the roof was purposely built with a curve to enable the slats to knit more closely together and reduce the risk of lifting by wind, particularly on high exposed buildings.

# Drystone Walling

IN a region where stone was easily obtained it was cheaper to enclose fields with walls (Pls 207–11) than by planting hedges; moreover, on the high bare wolds young quicksets given no protection from the persistent tugging winds would have found it difficult to keep a roothold in the light stony brash.

Cotswold differs from other districts where stone is used for boundary walls because of the tractable nature of oolitic limestone and because it comes out of the quarries in layers, so that the work to be done on the raw material is considerably lessened. The drystone walls of the Pennines and other northern districts are built of rough heavy boulders of irregular shapes not easily worked into neat blocks, making the structure coarse and heavy. Good workmanship is there but the result is less pleasing to the eye because the stone is difficult to work; the flakes of Cotswold stone lend themselves more readily to the waller's skill and their colour and texture blend more kindly into the landscape. The walls do not obscure the rolling lines of the wolds but seem to ride along with them.

Drystone walling has always been a Cotswold trade, from the days when Neolithic men built the horned entrance of the chambered long barrow of Belas Knap until today. For there has been a magnificent revival with the new prosperity and on the hills one can now see long new lengths replacing the old crumbling walls, many of which date back to the Enclosures. The time of its greatest increase was the eighteenth century with the passing of the Enclosure Acts, and then again in the bad times of the nineteenth when the big landowners had miles of walls erected about their estates, often to provide work for the unemployed.

One finds some of the best examples of drystone walling in the districts where roofing slates were quarried in large quantities in the old days, for example around Eyford and the Guitings. Here the stone is found in thin layers and the debris from the slate making, the thin flakes which had to be cleared before the pendle was reached, provided excellent material for wallers, the flat rectangles fitting so closely on top of each other that there is barely room for a mouse to squeeze through. It was not necessary for the walls to be as strong or as high as those of northern

England, for the old Cotswold breed of sheep were less agile than the hardier mountain sheep of the north, and more docile. Binding the stones with mortar has little advantage, though of recent years the toppers or combers, placed upright and slightly slanting to finish off the top of a wall, have been cemented, the main reason being the increase in vandalism and the theft of toppers by townsfolk to make rockeries. Mortar tends to hold rainwater, while the open spaces between the stones provide ventilation to the wall and keep the stones dry.

The waller's tools are few and have changed little since the Middle Ages: a mason's hammer, a pick and a crowbar, the hammer being heavy and boat-shaped and used for rough dressing the stones. The course is set with a tight string, one end fastened in the existing piece of wall with the other end attached to the wooden frame shaped in outline to the transverse section of the wall.

Foundations are dug out, usually only a few inches until fairly solid rock is found, and then large blocks roughly dressed are laid in the shallow cavity. A heap of large blocks is kept at one side for insertion at irregular intervals as the courses begin to rise; these are called jumpers or throughers and are part of the interlocking system holding the wall together. A run of seven yards or so is laid at a time, that is practically a week's work, according to William Pulham of Lower Oddington who reckoned nine yards, which included pulling down and using old stone. In Rudge's time the cost was five shillings a perch including all expenses.

One waller explained to me that to provide a good bond the rule was one stone on two and two on one, to wedge each stone with smaller pieces to keep it firm, and to keep the middle filled up as one went along to reinforce the two outer faces. A drystone wall consists of two outer walls starting on a base thickness of about two feet and tapering upward to about sixteen inches, the interior filled with stone debris and coarse rubble. Although many work alone, when a waller is being paid by the length an assistant makes it possible almost to double his speed. In the old days he often took his wife and children along, and while he built the faces one handed him the chips for pinning the stone and the others filled in the centre.

To the experienced waller each stone has its place, and I have watched men selecting stones with what seemed time-wasting scrutiny, and listened to their wry comments on the quarry which had provided such poor walling stone. In the past, good quarrymen put aside stone for drystone walling, but this type of quarry grows scarcer each year and a stone waller today often has to make do with a load of rough stone and make his own selection from it.

I have never found a waller who could explain to me why he selected one stone and not another which looked much the same in size; they learned the job by experience and by imbibing knowledge of the trade from the older men who originally trained them and in some cases, I feel sure, had an inherited, instinctive understanding impossible to put into words.

Methods vary a little in different parts of the Cotswolds, as do the colour and quality of the stone. There are different kinds of drystone walls for different purposes: the boundary wall around an estate, for example, was a more highly finished job than field walls, with the mason providing dressed stones for gate posts or gate pillars and the walls ending flush to them, while the whole of the wall would be built of evenly dressed stones or have courses of squared ones. Garden walls are sometimes given special treatment of neatly assembled layers made of stones of the same size, with rounded topping of cement instead of the slanting loose toppers.

In the eighteenth century and earlier farm buildings were sometimes erected with walls of drywalling, an outer and inner face with a rubble interior, and some can still be seen today. Often the interstices of the outside walls have been filled with mortar at a later date, and the interior roughly surfaced, probably to provide a drier store though the ventilation given by the crevices must have helped to keep the interior dry. Too much earth mixed with the rubble infilling meant walls that became damp whenever the atmosphere was humid. The barns and smaller outhouses I have seen with walls of drystone have all been made with small dressed stones roughly the size of standard bricks or smaller, and these have fitted so closely that the adhesion between the rough surfaces of the stones and the weight of each layer made mortar between the joints unnecessary to keep the wall firm and upright.

However toughened and leathery a waller's hands they suffered in cold wet weather, for the sharp shell fragments in the stone cut the hard skin and the lime in the stone dried up the natural oils so that the skin cracked, leaving painful open cuts. They had several homemade salves for this mostly made out of pig fat, but one man I knew swore by kipper skin and if his wife did not provide this delicacy at least once a week for his evening meal she was in trouble. I thought he was teasing me about this—a countryman has his own way of countering questions from inquisitive people—but I asked his wife and she assured me that she was never allowed to throw away the skins of the kippers or the fat from the pan in which she had cooked them. Her regret was that this robbed the cat of a tasty morsel.

# Woodcraft

## THE HURDLE-MAKER

UNLIKE most country craftsmen the hurdle-maker (Pls 216–221) did not suffer a decline with the advent of modern sheep farming; the shepherd still needed hurdles to fold his sheep and barbed wire and electric fences are useless as windbreaks. In recent years he has found another type of customer, retired people who have taken over the old cottages and who buy his wattle fencing to enclose their gardens for a stricter privacy than the villagers in the old days found necessary or could afford.

Hurdle-making was never big business but like other country trades was carried on by a family or a man on his own who bought up the timber in a coppice each season, cut his own poles and used the remainder for other forms of woodcraft. Rick pegs, for instance, the willow stakes cleft and then sharpened at one end with a few blows of the billhook, were made out of odds and ends left over from hurdle-making and filled in time when other business was slack. In the days of thatched ricks the hurdle-maker could sell as many as he had on hand, for the thatching must be done quickly to protect the gathered crop before the weather damaged it. Making rick pegs looks a simple, almost leisurely, job, but there is expertise in the neat flicks of the hook. One old man I used to watch had the same economy of movement of all manual workers as they grow older, no wasted effort or wasted energy.

This old man was over eighty and crippled with rheumatism, but so that he could continue working to the end, as he did, had taught himself to keep everything neat and in its right place in and about the open-fronted workshop adjoining his cottage. A pile of ash and willow poles was ready in one corner, while his tools on a heavy homemade bench stood to hand. There was always the smell of green wood in the shed. 'The greener the wood the better I likes it, easier to work', he said, and explained about the pegknots, those scars on the poles where there had been side branches. These made splitting the poles more difficult, but he had to take what he could get, coppice wood having been neglected for years. He no longer owned a coppice of his own but was dependent upon one he rented from a local farmer, who had let his men cut firing and fence stakes in the wood without supervision and 'they made a proper mess on it', not understanding how to take wood from a coppice without ruining it for others. Lack of proper cutting and grading could spoil a coppice for years.

He went on to tell me how in the old days basket-makers, hurdle-makers, carpenters who made ladders and hay-racks, each understood how to cut timber from a coppice, the ash and hazel from the stools every ten years or so, wands from the pollarded willows every three years to thin them but leaving half of the wands to grow to a good size for as long as eight years. 'Each on us knew what was hissun, we helped each other,' he said. And it came to me how many times I had heard that expression when talking to elderly villagers about the old days.

The poles were partially trimmed on the spot and the hurdle-maker usually set up a rough shelter amongst the trees to get a little protection from the weather. By doing as much as he could in the wood transport was lessened. After being sawn into the required lengths the poles were cleft with a long-headed slender axe, probably made by the village blacksmith, the split being started by standing the pole upright and driving the tool into the top with a wooden beetle. A device used for further splitting consisted of three upright poles with crossbars which gripped the pole firmly as the hurdle-maker held the cleft open with one hand while with the other he pushed the axe up the middle of the pole, gradually splitting it throughout its length. A few finishing touches with a knife and the material was ready to be made into hurdles. These actions were performed deftly and with a certain concentration and a faint motion of satisfaction as his guiding hand finished each pole. There was no sense of urgency but a slow working rhythm.

The hurdle-maker had a special tool made by the local smith, a tool which another hurdle-maker, Mr Arthurs, called a tommyhawk. This had a short thick hooked nose at right angles at one end, part of an old horse rake tine, and he used this for squaring up the oblong holes, made by boring with a bit, for the rails to pass through, a job hard on chisels and needing a specially tempered tool.

The kind of hurdle made for the farmer is the gate hurdle which, as its name implies, resembles a fivebarred gate and whose design has changed little since it was first evolved. The average size is six foot long and three feet high with extended pointed ends for inserting the hurdle into the ground. The uprights are thicker than the bars, with holes made in them to receive the tapered ends of the six bars used for each hurdle. A vertical brace placed midway and two diagonals from the outer bottom corners to the top centre keep the hurdle rigid, the pliable cleft wood making it resilient. The bars are placed at distances decreasing from top to bottom, to prevent sheep and lambs escaping from the fold. At lambing time when the shepherd builds his pens, bales of straw are added to make solid walls to keep out the wind and weather.

My old friend had only taken to making wattles in the last few years of his life. They were made of hazel and paid him better, and he showed me a long block of wood, cut from a tree trunk with a slight curve in it, in which he had bored ten equally spaced holes, into which he put the upright rods called 'shores'. The curve in the block was necessary and he told me how he had searched through the wood for a tree with just this gentle bend.

Having inserted the uprights he then wove the cleft pliable hazel wands in and out of the staves, and when he came to the outer end the wand had to be given a half-twist and turn before he went on with the return weaving. Great care must be taken to see the fibres in the grain are not broken, and this is the trickiest part of the job, for a novice at least, as I realized when I tried and found I could not bend the wand sufficiently to make a neat turn until exerting all my strength I broke the fibres and had to begin again. As each long runner comes to an end a fresh one is put in and the weaving continued until the whole set of uprights are covered. The wattle is then taken out of its tree-trunk frame and the ends neatly trimmed off. Then the end shores, longer than those inside, are chopped into points ready to be hammered into the ground. When taken off the block the wattles show a slight curve, but when stacked they straighten under their own weight. The curve is a device whereby the wattle is tightened a little; woven completely straight it would slacken. When wattles are made for a farmer an unwoven space is often left in the centre so that a stick can be thrust through and a number be carried easily.

The making of hurdles for sheep-folding has been an essential Cotswold craft since the Enclosures; wattle-making must be one of the most ancient, as can be seen by the impression left by them on clay and other substances on prehistoric sites, and it has persisted ever since. Medieval wattling is still in existence and one could trace it throughout each century to our own.

Many of the old coppices and narrow belts and triangles of rough woodland where the hurdle-maker once cut his material have vanished, some of them when lanes and their junctions have been widened, for a strip of mixed woodland rather like a wide untrimmed hedge was often left as a windbreak for the fields beyond, and others have been lost with the coming of the combine harvester and prairie type farming. Indiscriminate felling of hillside woods has destroyed much of the economy of the old woodland crafts where ordered felling in the old days meant renewal, not death. As well as long poles cut to lengths for special purposes there were pieces for the shorter handles of billhooks and cleavers, bundles of faggots for the bread ovens, bramble trails for ties, spars for thatchers, and firewood and kindling for all; nothing was wasted and the coppice was kept clean.

There have always been solitary hurdle-makers who preferred to work in the woods, making a rough shelter of hurdles and straw, with a small fire kept burning outside his hut to consume the waste and boil his kettle. But with the coming of the motor car and picnic parties looking for secluded spots off the road these men are disappearing. Unlike the shepherd alone on a hill with his flock, who welcomes a visitor, the few hurdle-makers I have met working in the woods have been gruff and unwelcoming to strangers and obviously uneasy until one left their territory. After setting up his shelter he first erects a chopping post and the row of poles to provide a gauge for the various lengths he needs, in autumn and winter felling and splitting the rods and in the spring and summer making the hurdles.

Today the hurdle-maker spends a few weeks in late autumn gathering material and chopping the poles into lengths, and then carts them back to the workshop, where the timber is stacked until he is ready to use it.

One man also made besoms which he sold in the local market. He seemed quite willing to talk about them. He bought the twigs from 'Hereford way' because birch twigs are best for the job and there is not a lot of birch grown on Cotswold. He told me lady gardeners bought them and that he always used one himself. 'They seem to be coming back. One time nobody wanted them, now I could sell as many and more as I can make. But I don't put meself out', he added, giving me a sudden grin.

I asked him to make me one as he had sold his present stock. And could I watch him doing it? This was rather a problem and he ruminated over it, but he agreed when I told him there was nothing better for sweeping leaves and wormcasts from the lawn. There was no doubt he was enthusiastic about them and my remark pleased him. I thought that making a besom entailed a handful of twigs with a stout pole thrust inside and made fast with a wire band but he explained he never used wire but a cleft hazel rod or a piece of bramble stem. He had a special tool for the job, a bramble hook, bought at a farm sale years ago for a few pence; the first owner used bramble for tying his sheaves, he told me.

All the time he was working he was talking to me, first cutting a pole into the right length and shaving it at both ends. Then he took an armful of springy twigs from a bundle, arranged them with the longest ones outside, thrust the stick in the middle and secured it with a pliable piece of cleft willow. 'Try this for size', he said. 'A good besom should have a bit of a curve in it. It saves your back.'

As soon as I began to sweep I realized how easy it felt. 'It's the first time I ever had a besom made to measure', I told him, delighted not only with the besom but with the kindly thought for my comfort. I asked him how he had learnt to make them. 'From an old chap who worked for my Dad when I was a nipper. We had the run of Poor's Lot, a nice little wood that was. This old chap ud' turn up in the autumn and Dad let him have the brushwood and poles for help with the felling. There was some birch and willow at the bottom end where it was marshy. Dad didn't want the birch; he was a hurdle-maker.'

My new friend went on to tell me how the old man cut the heads of the young birch and put them in bundles, some crossways and some lengthwise, building the bundles into a kind of ridge so the rain would run off. Then off he would go until the spring and they would find him there making his brooms on an old tree trunk he called his besom horse, where he had fixed a sort of vice to hold one end of the willow wand while he tied on the twigs. When he had made a few dozen besoms he would be off again. While he was making the besoms he lived rough in the wood, not in the hurdle-maker's shelter but one he had made for himself under the hedge.

'Did he cook for himself?' I asked.

'There was a good smell coming from his cooking pot,' was the reply. 'But if he helped himself to a rabbit or a bird he never left no signs of feathers or fur or signs of a snare. Dad warned him when he first come, the squire wouldn't stand for poaching, but hardly a soul knew he was in the wood he went about so quiet and secret, like a shadder when he wasn't working.'

'Where did he come from?' I asked.

'He never told us and we never asked,' was the reply.

There is a bramble hook in George Swinford's museum in Filkins, the head about four inches long with a steel tip. Mr Swinford told me it had belonged to a local farmer who used bramble ties for his sheaves, first putting the trails through a ring to remove the thorns and then splitting them before they were hung up ready for use.

### FIELD GATES

Field gates, until the wholesale introduction of metal gates, were made by the local carpenter, wheelwright or timber merchant. The traditional pattern on Cotswold differed from other districts by having wooden latches, and around the Paxford-Ebrington district these can still be seen (Pls 222, 223). The wood, elm or oak, is silvery grey and toughened and scarred with age, but the gates are still serviceable, examples of a style now obsolete. Where new field gates are made of wood mass-produced metal fasteners have taken the place of the wooden latch.

# The Thatcher

ALTHOUGH the majority of Cotswold buildings were roofed with stone slates, in the villages bordering Worcestershire and Warwickshire one can still find groups of thatched cottages and a number whose original thatched roofs have been replaced by grey artificial tiles. At Ebrington, for instance, massive stone buttresses on several cottages reveal the fact that their roofs were once thatched, for when it was decided to re-roof them with tiles and the old roof was taken off, the walls began to sag and had to be buttressed before the heavier tiled roof could be put on.

The farmer, of course, always needed thatchers for his corn or hay ricks, though these were sometimes thatched by men who worked on the farm, any of whom could do most jobs when necessary; and there were gangs who went from farm to farm whose sole job was thatching ricks.

The craft is one of great antiquity and the method has changed little down the centuries. Today it has become a specialized job, and once again, after a decline, thatchers are in demand by retired people coming into the villages and wanting to preserve or enhance the picturesque appearance of their modernized cottages. Many of them, however, prefer Norfolk reed as more lasting than local wheat straw. In any case it is difficult to obtain the right kind of straw nowadays, though a few farmers harvest their wheat in the old way to meet the new demand, and find that it pays. At one time, before combine harvesters were common, the wheat growing round the outside of a field was cut with sickle or scythe to make way for the reaper or binder and the long straw thus obtained was used for thatching.

Different counties and districts have their own methods of preparing the reeds or straw but when it was used on Cotswold, not a district where thatch was the customary roofing material, it took the simplest form. In the nineteenth century the materials and workmanship were pretty much the same for the cottages as for the ricks. A landowner beautifying his estate cottages might insist upon straw reeds and a more elaborate finish at the eaves, and an occasional customer with his own ideas might not trouble about the extra cost, but on the whole a watertight roof, not the appearance, was the aim. Indeed some of the farmers were probably prouder of their ricks than of their workers' cottages and liked to see them finished off with straw ornaments or 'dollies', whereas it never occurred to them to finish off a cottage with a straw finial in the same way as a Cotswold builder liked to finish off his gables with a small carved stone ornament. The custom of adding a straw long-tailed bird to the roof-ridge of a thatched cottage is a modern embellishment introduced from outside.

The thatcher's tools are a wooden mallet for driving in the spars; needles of various sizes for holding the yealms in position and for sewing the tarred string in the thatch; a bow, or reed-holder, which can be hooked on the roof to hold a bundle of straw while thatching; a 'yack', or yoke, that is, a forked implement of wood to carry the yealms to the roof; a spar hook for splitting and pointing hazel rods; an eaves hook, a short-handled knife; and an eaves knife; side-rake and hand shears (Pl. 227).

Knee pads and ladders are also part of his equipment and, as always, individual craftsmen have their own special tools made or adapted for them and evolved out of experience.

# Small Industries

DURING the great expansion of trade in the late eighteenth and nineteenth centuries before industry had settled into its own factory areas and steam was still a new source of power for driving machinery a number of old mills on Cotswold previously used for fulling or grinding turned over to paper-making. In those days mills were an asset and not a blight upon the countryside, providing work for village people at a time when the cloth trade had fallen away and agriculture could not absorb all the rural population.

Cotswold, with its many small streams and rivers providing both power and clean pure water for the process, was ideal for the new manufacture of paper-making. There were workpeople available in the villages and during a period of roughly 150 years, between 1750 and 1900, there were some twenty-nine paper mills started in Gloucestershire and probably more, records of many small ones having completely vanished except for farm names such as Paper Mill Farm near Stanway, or Paper Mill cottages, once Hound Mill on the Windrush at Barrington where paper-making was carried on between 1816 and 1846 by George Ward. One finds Paper Mills mentioned in Excise Letters, or in a newspaper of the period recording an accident or sale, but that is all.

The coming of paper-making machinery, the duties on paper, easier transport, the changes in the sources and kinds of raw material and the competition of large concerns in urban industrial districts saw the end of most of the paper mills in remote country districts. These had been small family affairs specializing in a particular kind of paper, using water to power their plant and without much capital to invest in the new machinery which enabled paper to be made more cheaply and more quickly. The mill sites, many of them going back to Domesday as corn or fulling mills, were once more left to their solitudes or were taken over as grinding mills for animal feeding stuffs, until these in their turn became uneconomic with the rise of big business. A few managed to survive and prosper by keeping up with new methods. The Postlip Mills, for example, near Winchcombe, by specializing

in filter papers for use in industry, laboratories and hospitals made itself an important place in the paper-making industry and its history, written by Eleanor Adlard,
is a fascinating study of the growth of an industry for nearly two hundred years,
showing the progression from its early years when the paper was dried in lofts
fitted with wooden-slatted sides, the air through the slats being regulated according
to the weather and drying time best suited to the type of paper, to the introduction of
up-to-date drying plants. These lofts with large wooden-slatted openings are one
of the indications today that a building was once a paper mill. The old drying loft
at Middle Mill, Postlip, has now disappeared together with the stone shed in front
of it which had the date 1834 and the initials G.N. on a circular plaque, but at
Little Barrington one can still see the remains of a drying loft, with some of the
slats in position and obvious signs on an outside wall where openings have been
filled in when the mill became Paper Mill Cottages.

Quenington, on the Coln, had one of the earliest paper mills. The *Gloucester
Journal* of 14th February 1791 records the death of a Mr Joshua Carby, who died in
1791 aged 84, 'an eminent paper maker and a honest man'. There is a paper mill
marked on Taylor's Map of Gloucestershire, 1777, and Rudder in 1779 notes that
writing paper was made in Quenington and that the mill employed a few hands. The
mill was working at least until 1860, according to the Paper Mill Directory of
that year.

Several of the cloth mills of South Cotswold were adapted for paper-making
though none survived for very long and the number of people who found employment in them made little difference to the unemployment problem prevailing when
the cloth mills went out of business. Hack Mill, at Wotton under Edge, a mill
going back at least to the days of Kingswood Abbey for it is mentioned in the 1537
Lease Book of the Abbey, and John Smith, the Berkeley historian, mentions it as
coming into an Exchequer Plea of 1613, was advertised for sale in 1774 as a 'very
complete and newly erected paper mill'.

We know very little about these mills, that is their daily working and output,
except in the case of Postlip Mill, near Winchcombe, where there are still a few
retired employees who remember the old days and some of the processes from their
own working days or the days of their parents, and they recall the benevolent
paternalism of the firm with affection and nostalgia. A job at Postlip Mills was a
job for life; some worked there for over fifty years. One of the oldest, Mrs Nightingale, walked to and from Winchcombe daily for sixty-six years. The Lishmans,
father and son, put in a hundred years and it is said that Alf Lishman was the last
to wear the paper cap of blue sample paper once worn by all the men at the mill and
which they folded themselves. The life of Winchcombe was bound up with its

prosperity and many an old Winchcombe family, the Okeys, Scatters, Mason, Yeend and Nightingale families, worked there. The Adlard family who ran the mill followed in the tradition of the old woolmen, that is some of the profits spilled over into the church and the building of almshouses for retired workers as well as the renovating and building of new cottages for the workers.

## THE SILK TRADE

Another small industry which came to Cotswold because of the plentiful supply of pure water was the silk ribbon trade, and like the manufacture of paper it had a life of about 150 years, less in some villages. On the whole these industries left little mark on the region; they gave employment during the hungry years of the late nineteenth century when agriculture could no longer absorb the population and the cloth mills had closed down and they left behind a few pleasant stone mill structures and rows of workers' cottages.

In the Blockley and Campden districts the silk trade was a subsidiary of the Coventry manufacture, started in the villages because of a supply of cheap labour and copious water. One of the earliest mills was built in Blockley by Henry Whatcott in 1700 (Pl. 230), where throwing, cleaning and preparing the raw silk for dyers and weavers to make into ribbons was carried on, one of the latest was at Campden, on the Mill Stream, and dates from early nineteenth century. The Campden silk mill, like the others, was forced to give up with the advent of Free Trade, but the building continued to be used as a glove and stay-making mill until it was finally taken over by Ashbee's Guild of Craftsmen in 1901 and it is still occupied by one of a famous family of silversmiths today.

Blockley rises steeply from the narrow valley holding Knee Brook, the chief source of water for the mills, which begins in Bourton Wood beyond Dovedale. There is little flat space in the village and the buildings are sited on narrow shelves at different levels, the terrain lending itself to long terraces of cottages rather than individual dwellings. Springs gush out from the various heights above the valley; until much of the water was piped at source there was always the sound of water in Blockley. The fact that the village has strata of buildings in its bright yellow stone gives it a distinctive air, the terraces and long low mills going along in the line of the flow of its rock.

Today the mills and cottages left by the silk trade blend well with the rest of the village. The mills have been turned into country houses, with the mill stream providing charming water-gardens. One which houses several families is situated just below the church, with the wide reservoir an ornamental water edged with reeds and rushes and its far side holding tall dark trees out of which the orange buff of the church tower rises like one of those planned landscapes of the eighteenth century; the long rectangular building has settled with grace into the valley. The frontage is plain, but the good masonry pleases the eye; the builder had not forgotten the tradition of good workmanship though he did not express it in the vernacular.

Unfortunately the silk-throwing depended on the ribbon trade of Coventry and when the demand for silk ribbons declined the subsidiary factories were the first to go out of business. When under the 1860 Treaty between France and England the duty of 30 per cent was taken off foreign ribbons and they were admitted free into this country while France and other countries still kept high protective duties, English manufacturers were ruined, thousands of workers lost their jobs and their homes. In Coventry at this time there were more paupers than workers, the loss of the silk mills affecting not only the workers but shopkeepers and other tradesmen as well. There were strikes and other disturbances in Coventry; in the Cotswold villages as the silk mills closed down and no other work was available there were again the sad exodus to look for other work and the familiar tightening of belts, for the women and children who had supplied the bulk of the labour in the mills had also provided the main earning power of the family. The situation was so bad in the winter of 1860-1 that a parochial meeting was held to discuss the situation on 15th January 1861, for the purpose of relieving the distress which was increased by the severity of the weather.

After the outbreak of war between France and Prussia in the summer of 1870, when trade with France was halted, the mills of Blockley started to work again, but the war over, France soon recovered and silk ribbons began to come into the country duty free. By 1875 only two mills in Blockley, worked by Charles Edwin Smith and George Stanley and employing about 200 people, continued to function, but these were finally obliged to shut down.

A small collar-making business started in 1866 by a London firm provided work for a few women once employed in the silk mills, starting in a house with ten sewing machines and employing about thirty people, the number increasing to fifty. Smith's Mill was then used with sixty or more outworkers making buttonholes in shirt fronts, but this second attempt to turn Blockley into an industrial centre also failed. It left no visible mark upon the village but it seems likely that these excursions into industry, the exploitation of its women and children had something to do with its old reputation as a radical village in the heart of a Conservative stronghold.

The closing of the mills brought about the closing of the school provided for the children aged between eight and eleven under a provision of the Factory Act that all children employed must attend school during part of the day. The school was entirely controlled by the mill-owners until 1861 when, business being bad, they withdrew their support for the school and it was discontinued.

## PIANO-MAKING

Two small piano factories were started at the end of the century, but they lasted only until 1910. They were small concerns and employed only a few men, the bulk of the work being performed by the owners. In those days a new piano cost around £10, and pianos made by John Ocock & Son and by Evans & Evans at Sleepy Hollow Mill were practically handmade and of excellent quality. Few, unfortunately, survive today.

John Ocock was a woodcarver, and the fretted front panels were his own work from the selecting of the wood to the last finishing touches. He had a local reputation as a woodcarver and in 1910 he received the commission to make the presentation casket for the ceremony of conferring the Freedom of the Borough of Stratford-upon-Avon to the famous actor-manager Sir Frank Benson. The oak for the casket came from Shottery.

Looked at in retrospect, the Old Mill with its trout stream only a few feet away in the quiet of the countryside seems an idyllic place in which to make pianos, and work there must have been very pleasant. It was not a large concern, and included John Ocock's son, Alfred. A pleasant family business, never making a fortune, with none of the haste and bustle of a money-making epoch, the kind of business, in fact, that would be considered uneconomic, almost criminal today, yet it provided a sufficient livelihood for a few families and caused little disturbance to the peace of the countryside.

The other piano firm, Evans & Evans, was also run by a wood carver, the late Richard Pain, who was also an excellent pianist and tuner. I doubt if one could find an Ocock or an Evans piano in Blockley today; when I enquired I was told of their pianos appearing at local auctions and being sold for a few shillings for piano-smashing contests or even to be chopped up for firewood.

Blockley with its many attempts to become an industrial centre could be seen as an example of how in the last years of the nineteenth century the urge to start new businesses had spilled over into the countryside, where in spite of the new sources of power for machinery coming into fashion the old mill using water-power was still cheaper and where labour was plentiful and cheap. The silk mills failed because the Treaty between France and England was abrogated, then the collar trade, which also included shirt fronts, had taken over Smith's Mill. Sleepy Hollow Mill became a piano factory to take advantage of the fashion of the time that every house should possess a piano, while Good Intent Mill became a paper mill for a short period. Cheshire's Mill, Daddy Lowe's Mill and Turvey's Mill turned to corn and cider, and another became a factory for the making of liquid soap at the turn of the century. Whatever the reason, lack of capital, lack of demand for the products, an inadequate understanding of the market, by the turn of the century most had ceased to be worked and Blockley's bid to be an industrial centre came to an end. I doubt if the people who live in the district today feel any regrets when they compare its clear brooks and streams, its green hillsides and encircling woodlands with the industrial districts of the Midlands and the north of England. Indeed, amongst its inhabitants today are many who have fled from those places.

# 5

# VILLAGE FEASTS AND PASTIMES

*'No one of reflective mind can possibly separate the old-world
cottage from the lives once lived in it.'*

# Village Feasts and Pastimes

## CLUB WALKING

THE holiday of the year belonging entirely to the village, a holiday not given by the government, squire or church, was the Whitsuntide Feast and Club Walking. By the middle of the nineteenth century the ancient spring festival, the patronal day, the day each year when the town or village had been granted a charter to hold a market in the Middle Ages, all these occasions in many instances had been blended into or superseded by the Club or Feast Day. Every village had its holiday, which was often extended to three days, and the principal event, the men's dinner, was paid for by the men, who for the past twelve months had paid a few pence into the Club each week. Broadway had one day, Whit Monday, when a marquee was erected for a Roast Beef dinner for the men belonging to the Coach and Horses Sick and Dividend Club, and the women and children did not share this treat; Sid Knight in his *Cotswold Lad* describes how with other boys he used to hang about the marquee sniffing the good smells.

Ebrington had three days' holiday and this was shared by the whole village, the men's dinner on the first day, a tea-party for the women and children on the second day and the third to go visiting friends and relations in the neighbourhood. There were swings and roundabouts under the Oaks, stalls selling sweets and cakes, and dancing at night in the street to fiddle and melodion. After a short service in the church there was the grand parade through the village with banners and the village band paying courtesy calls on the vicar, the farmers and such local gentry as might be expected to provide free drinks. The women and children followed the procession in their best dresses and I was told that every shade of white appeared in their clothes from the ivory tint of old wedding dresses to the snowy white pinafores of the children. The men wore their best suits, kept especially for funerals, weddings and Club days, often the one best suit they owned during their adult life and this made the elderly men look unfamiliar and sometimes uncomfortable, particularly those whose figures had changed since the suit was made. Daughters in service in the towns tried to get home for this holiday and were noticeable because of the more fashionable cut of their clothes. In one village in south Cotswold an old man, known as Soapy Sam because soap was a commodity he never used, always begged a piece of suet for cleaning his boots before Club Day, the only time they were cleaned if local gossip can be believed. Stories about his dirty habits were stock jokes in the village trotted out at the pub to amuse the visitor, and these stories pursued the poor man to his last days, for being taken to hospital after a serious fall he was supposed to have been heard protesting loudly on being undressed and bathed, that he never washed what was 'kivered', and that a bath would kill him. He died the day after being admitted.

The week before the holiday was devoted to spring cleaning the houses and cottages, a clearing away of the soot and grime of winter; one old lady told me she could remember not only the walls being whitewashed but the steps and forecourts as well. Everything that could be washed went into the tub, and those who could afford a new outfit or part of one sported it for this occasion. It might be only a new sash or last summer's hat retrimmed.

The dinner, which was cooked at the pub, was a generous one, roast beef, lashings of vegetables and a plum pudding to follow, with as much bread and cheese, beer and cider as they wanted. In those days when wages were low a good meal was something to be appreciated; many farm workers seldom had roast meat except at Christmas, when a joint of beef was a bonus from the farmer, or when they killed a pig, though pigmeat was too precious for much of it to be roasted. Cold fat bacon, cheese, bred and vegetables from the garden or allotment were their daily fare—that is, the men had the bacon while the women and children had bread sometimes spread with lard from the pig, and a thin slice of bacon on a mound of cabbage for a special treat.

The original banner of the Ebrington Men's Club was discovered a few years ago in the cottage of an old man who once helped to carry it in the Whit Thursday procession. It measures several yards in width and is of royal blue silk, painted on each side with the words 'Ebrington Friendly Society' 'Instituted September 29th, 1856', and 'Let Brotherly Love Continue' in black letters on golden scrolls. Each side also has a painted picture, one depicting the Good Samaritan with the words 'Go and do Likewise'. On the other side are five figures representing farm workers holding a rope tied round the stump of a tree, and at their feet a sickle, pick, shovel and rake, the symbols of their trades, with the words 'Unity is Strength' on a golden scroll beneath the picture, obviously symbolizing that they must all pull together; and a wreath of oak leaves enclosing a pair of clasped hands. The name of the maker, well known at this period for making banners, G. Tutil, 63 City Road, London, appears on both sides of the banner.

An old photograph, of around 1900 (Pl. 238), of the Club procession shows two smaller banners being carried, one with the arms of Lord Ebrington, the other of the Earl of Harrowby, the two chief landlords of the village. It would be interesting to know when the two smaller banners were added to the handsome original with its hand-painted pictures and messages of brotherly love evidently made when the agricultural labourer was beginning to realize that unity could be strength.

The First World War brought the Club Walking to an end. Like many other village institutions it was discontinued during the war years and was not started up again because the young men who should have kept the tradition alive never came back, and for those who did the old way of life was no longer valid. But older villagers still remember with pleasure those old days of communal festivity. One old lady over ninety told me with her eyes sparkling with pleasure: 'I wore out a good pair of shoes on the stones. I dearly loved a dance to a fiddle in those days.' She also told me that one reason why it was difficult to find the wooden staffs that were topped with ornate brass knobs and carried by the men in the procession was that when a man died they would break his staff and put it in his coffin, but this custom was dying out when she was a girl. One can still see occasionally the brass knobs which topped the staffs on cottage mantelshelves, kept in memory of a relative who owned it.

Whitsun Thursday seems to have been the usual day in the north Cotswold for the feast to begin, and in some villages large boughs of oak were hung outside the inns and beerhouses.

The bellringers of every parish church had their own smaller Feast after ringing the bells in memory of the escape of King and Parliament from the Gunpowder Plot. Ebrington's Churchwardens' Accounts going back as far as 1793 show they were paid six shillings every 5th November, and this lasted well into the nineteenth century.


MAY WALKING

May Day celebrations have the flavour of great antiquity, but it is difficult today to disentangle true survivals from the many attempts at revival since the Restoration. The years of Puritan rule disrupted these festivals and when they were renewed in the eighteenth and nineteenth centuries a hooligan element often crept in from surrounding industrial districts. The original festivals had their orgiastic side but there was reason behind them, or so those taking part believed, whereas later, the true purpose forgotten they degenerated into unseemly behaviour that the puritans of later centuries felt must be put down.

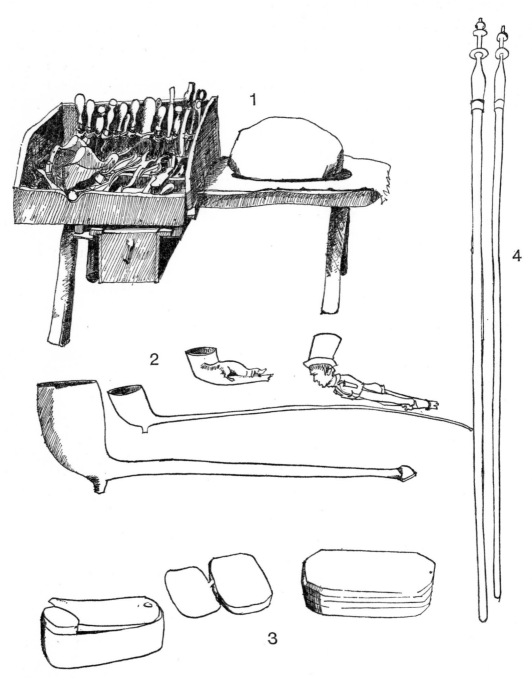

*1, Cobbler's bench with tools and lapstone; from Filkins Museum. 2, Clay pipes including pipes belonging to French prisoners of the Napoleonic Wars, and a cadger's pipe (the largest). 3, Tobacco tins. 4, Staffs for the banners carried on Club Day.*

We know a little of May Walking at Wotton under Edge from an account written by Vincent Perkins, who was born in 1830 and wrote about it in the years before 1850. Everyone, he said, went into the woods at five in the morning to gather young beech boughs before breakfast and it was considered unlucky not to do this. Any boy or girl who had no beech leaf to wear was jeered at and not allowed to join in the games that followed. Similar tales are told of Oak Apple Day all over the Midlands, an instance of the way old customs and traditions coalesce as the years go by.

Vincent Perkins also wrote about Cockshoot Fair, an ancient festival held in the Cockshoot ride of the woods on Westridge where there were shows and stalls presided over by a master weaver named Abbott, one of Wotton's well-known characters of the period. During the day the fun was orderly enough, but after dark waggons holding barrels of beer with men from all around would arrive, and then the excitement became intense as the men worked themselves up for the annual fight between Wotton and Nibley. This continued on Tuesday when they battled on Ley Hill, and on the third day a last rumbustious occasion, when the Benefit Club at Nibley was the objective. The fight over and the barrels empty, they returned home to mend their broken heads and relate their triumphs in the field to the stay-at-homes. This was brought to an end by the action of local clergy and residents appalled at the brutishness of much of the fighting, and by the fact that the clothing trade in Wotton and the surrounding districts had declined to such a pitch that the majority of the population was out of work; there was no money for feasts of any kind when most of the workers were starving or seeking work elsewhere.

## DOVER'S HILL GAMES AND OTHERS

The famous Dover's Hill Games, near Chipping Campden, also came to an end about this time. They, also, suffered from the gangs of hooligans who swarmed on to the hill, but the main reason why the games were abandoned was the Enclosure of the open fields of Weston Subedge, a late Act, when the plateau at the top of the hill where the games were held was awarded to various owners of rights in the common fields. The Dover's Hill Games have their own historian in Christopher Whitfield, and in a collection of verses by Drayton, Ben Jonson and some thirty other literary men of the period put together in 1639 under the title *Annalia Dubrensia*. The games took their name from Robert Dover, an attorney, who clad in garments once belonging to James I, and given by Endymion Porter of Aston Subedge, a servant of the king, first started them.

During the Civil War they were discontinued, and when they were revived they never again achieved the same fame. Dover was dead and the 'greater troops of gallants than Rome's street, Ere saw in Pompey's triumphs' had died also, either in battle for the king or of old age. Rudge says the games were poorly attended in 1800 but by 1820 'the great match of backswords, the wrestling, jingling, bowling, running in sacks, the pony racing and the dancing together with a multiplicity of Athletic Exercises and noted Cotswold Sports' as the handbill said, including Shin-kicking, were in full swing again for the three days of the games, accompanied by the booths selling ale and cider, sweets and gingerbread.

Backsword or Singlestick was played by two men trying to crack each other's skull, and it is said that with skilful players a match could last for ninety minutes, the prize being a guinea a couple, eighteen shillings for the winner and three for the loser, small compensation for a broken head.

Jingling required eight men, seven of whom entered a ring blindfolded while one with bells in his hands kept running about the ring. If caught in a certain time by one of the blindfolded man the captor gained a prize, but if the jingler escaped until the time expired the prize was his.

Shin kicking went on long after the Dover's Hill Games came to an end. Sid Knight describes it in *Cotswold Lad*. It was a test of endurance of pain rather than a sport and men prepared for it by a period of training, that is, they battered their shins or found someone else to batter them with hobnailed boots or a piece of planking until they were beaten into insensitivity. Mr Parnell of Ebrington explained to me how it was played when he was a boy. The two contestants had iron plates on the toes of their boots and, holding each other by the shoulders with outstretched arms, kicked at each other's shins until one was obliged to give in. Men who indulged in this pastime had scarred and corrugated shins and would pull up their trouser legs and show them as honourable scars. The champion's belt of the last sports on Dover's Hill depicts two men shin-kicking. Winchcombe was famous for its shin-kickers. If a man wanted a fight he would go to the Cross, throw up his hat and await a challenge.

A pastime of the villagers of Brockworth, to preserve their grazing rights on Cooper's Hill, was rolling wooden discs from the flagstaff at the top and catching them at the bottom, and the one who caught a disc won a cheese. This pastime still goes on today though it has lost much of its ancient significance. The discs represent cheeses, the famous Double Gloucester made in the vale below, and the sport has been known for the past five hundred years. The cheese rolling over, foot-races and other sports take place on the top of the hill.

There were small festivals in plenty unknown to the world outside. Cherry Wake

Sunday, at Saintbury, above the Vale of Evesham, whose inhabitants many years ago paid the rent with the money from the sale of their cherry orchards, and Cherry Fair, held on the last Sunday in June, in a cherry orchard in Synwell, Wotton under Edge, which went on well into the night with games and dancing. Pig's Face Sunday, at Avening in the south Cotswolds, was a special day when friends and relatives met to enjoy that delicacy, a kind of brawn made of the pig's cheeks and other small morsels of pork left after the remainder of the pig had been cut up. This was an autumn feast, after pig-killing.

Chipping Campden never had a particular day to eat its famous backbone pie, but it was always in the autumn after the cottage pig had been killed. It was eaten hot or cold but connoisseurs preferred it cold, and as a supper dish after church and a leisurely walk home it made a splendid finish to Sunday. Owing to the amount of bone and the small amount of meat inside the crust, the debris left on the plate could be a little embarrassing to a stranger, but once that was overcome the delicacy was thoroughly enjoyed. I used to be invited to a Backbone Pie supper in a farm where the farmer had an uncle who had been a regular soldier and who made his home at the farm after leaving the army. Each time I went I heard the same story and each time I enjoyed it. It seemed that Uncle when he was badly wounded had been asked by a kindly nurse if there was anything he fancied, for he had no appetite for hospital food. 'I told her she could bring me a chunk of backbone pie. She thought I was having her on, she'd never even heard of backbone pie!' And even after twenty years he had never quite got over his astonishment at finding someone who had never heard of backbone pie.

The annual Flower Show and Fete nowadays is the one occasion when the inhabitants of a village come together to enjoy themselves, but pleasant though it may be it has none of the compulsion of the old Club Day or Wake. Each year the organizers rack their brains to find new gimmicks to attract the crowds and persuade them to spend their money; in the old days an occasion when there was no work to do, plenty to eat and drink and neighbours and friends to share them with, an atmosphere of holiday and jollification, needed no gimmicks.

# A Cotswold Glossary

## A

**Archard,** orchard

**Ark,** corn bin divided into compartments for holding different kinds of grain for animal food

## B

**Balk,** banks of earth left between cultivated strips of land

**Banker,** stone work bench used by banker masons

**Banker masons,** men who cut cornices, mouldings, mullions, ornament, etc.

**Beam,** handle of breast plough

**Blowth,** fruit blossom

**Boffled,** worried

**Bolster,** cross-piece in front of undercarriage of waggon

**Bommux,** beat-up

**Bowsen,** lambing pen

**Brake,** three poles set upright on ground with connecting cross-bars to hold poles for splitting

**Brevet,** to search

**Burra,** hollow sheltered from the wind

## C

**Callous,** knot or obstruction in rock which prevents splitting

**Casalty,** changeable weather

**Cart-pad,** small wooden saddle-like device which takes the traces on ox-harness

**Chackle,** to chatter

**Chawl,** pig's cheek

**Chits,** long shoots on potatoes removed before planting

**Chumble,** to eat without teeth

**Chumper,** implement for cutting awns from barley used for poultry food

**Clomber,** to climb

**Combers,** large stones placed edgewise on top of drystone wall

**Comical,** out-of-sorts

**Corn-cradle,** device fitted to scythes to lay corn in neat swathes

**Cot-bowsen,** cottages

**Cradle,** wooden frame used for drystone walling

**Cruppers,** chains under the jaws of working oxen

**Cutlings,** coarse meal for pig food

## D

**Daddocky,** rotten wood

**Dandy-rolls,** device for making water-marks in paper

**Drawer,** one who repaired blemishes in new cloth before it was packed for sale

## E

**Ellern,** elder bush

**Ellum,** elm tree

# F

**Fammel,** famished
**Felt,** fieldfare
**Freddy,** tramp
**Frosted slates,** stone put out in winter to be
  split by frost into layers for slates
**Fuzz,** furse or whin

# G

**Galetting-torching,** stone chips put under roof
  slates from inside for swept valleys and places
  where rain might get in
**Glim,** light
**Gleer,** film of ice on road
**Gozzle grass,** goose grass
**Grandmother's whiskers,** plantain flowers

# H

**Hand-skim,** saucer-like ladle with holes for
  milk to drain through (Dairy)
**Hovels,** outhouses
**Humbledore,** bumblebee

# J

**Jad,** adze

# K

**Kibbling,** any method of coarse grinding
**Kind,** for a plant which thrives
**Kyaw,** stare
**Kyolloping,** pleased with oneself; strutting

# L

**Lands,** allotments, 22 yards wide, 10 chains long
**Langet,** field corridor

**Lattermath,** aftermath
**Lie-by,** bedfellow

# M

**Maggotty-pie,** magpie
**Masonter,** mason
**Mawkins,** slattern, mop-headed
**May-blobs,** Marsh marigolds
**Menagery,** used to describe odd collection of
  things or people
**Moil,** labour
**Mombly,** bewildered
**Moulter,** to melt
**Mounding,** hedge-laying
**Mullens,** chains on ox-harness
**Mullers,** rounded stones for grinding pig-
  ments—mainly for painting waggons
**Mullocky,** muggy
**Mumpus,** to fall mumpus—to fall flat

# N

**Nobble,** to eat

# O

**Off-shut,** lean-to shed
**Opple,** apple
**Ount,** mole
**Overburden,** top soil and stone brash removed
  before good stone is reached in quarrying

# P

**Pendle,** stone left out in open for frost to split
  before being made into slates
**Perishly,** withered
**Pikel,** pitchfork
**Pinnock,** small enclosure of land

**Plash,** small pool or ford

**Policeman,** single stook of corn left in field after harvest. No gleaning must begin until it is removed

**Potch,** basket used for fruit or vegetables

**Presents,** stone that splits naturally into layers without frosting

**Puller,** tool used by shepherds for taking up what remains of roots of mangolds after sheep have eaten them to the ground

# Q

**Quakers,** Quaking-grass (*Briza media*)

**Quarr,** quarry

**Quiddle,** fuss

**Quinet,** a wedge driven into pole-ring of scythe to hold it firm

**Quitch,** couch grass

**Quodlins,** red-cheeked apples

# R

**Rattleskull,** gooseberry wine

**Redding-up,** to make tidy

**Reever,** piece of wood fixed to wooden handle to draw pulp in cider press together

**Rowing,** drawing out loose fibres with teazles and raising nap on cloth

**Ruffing,** scratching on horse shoes to prevent a horse slipping on icy roads

**Rug-stone,** stone turned up by plough useless for masonry

**Runner,** bruising stone of cider-press

# S

**Sally,** willow-type of wood used for thatching and hurdle-making

**Scabbling axe,** tool used for rough dressing of stone

**Scathe,** damage

**Sharves,** cart shafts

**Sheep's-head clock,** wooden-faced wall-clock without a case

**Shift-stock,** tool used for the angles of bow windows

**Shuckers,** toppers finishing off drystone wall

**Shuckle,** hinge joining two parts of flail

**Shuppick,** pitchfork

**Skim-cut,** first pieces cut off to straighten block of stone

**Slats,** stone slates

**Slatter,** tiler

**Slice,** long-handled shovel

**Slip-slap gate,** turnstile

**Sloshetting,** walking through long wet grass

**Smith's breeze,** small coke for blacksmith's hearth

**Smullock,** all of a heap

**Snobberly,** cold in the head

**Spalt,** hammer-headed adze

**Staddle stones,** stones with triangular base and mushroom tops used as foundation for ricks, now mostly ornamental

**Strakes,** iron bands on waggon wheels

**Strickle or strick-stick,** stick used for levelling off corn in bushel measures

**Swinger,** brass disc suspended on ring on horse harness

**Swingle,** striking part of flail

# T

**Tallet,** loft over stables or similar outbuilding

**Tice,** coax or encourage

**Tenters,** hooks on which cloth was stretched to dry

**Thonky,** muggy

**Tingling-up,** propping up drystone wall in middle to compensate for natural sag

**Tod,** bale of fleeces—28 lb.

**Tommyhawk,** hurdle-maker's tool for squaring holes for rails to pass through

**Tongue-pole,** square pillow of wood—part of undercarriage of waggon

**Trow,** trough
**Track,** the proper hanging of a gate
**Tump,** hillock or ancient burial mound

# U

**Urchin,** hedgehog

# V

**Valley-stones,** slates used for swept valleys on roofs, triangular-shaped
**Varmints,** vermin

# W

**Wappered,** clogged-up
**Wain,** ox-cart
**Wave-wind,** bindweed
**Wimble,** implement for making straw rope

# Y

**Yawny,** simpleton
**Yolk,** natural grease of fleece
**Yowes,** ewes

# Bibliography

## PRINCIPAL SOURCES

Adlard, E., *History of Postlip Mills*.

Arkell, W. J., *Oxford Stone*. Faber, 1948.

Churchwardens' Accounts, Ebrington, 1793–1912.

*Gloucestershire Studies*. Leicester University Press, 1957.

Grundy, G. B., *Saxon Charters and Field Names of Gloucestershire*. Bristol and Gloucestershire Archaeological Society, 1935–6.

Jewson, Norman, *By Chance I Did Rove*. Sapperton, 1952.

Knapp, J. L., *Journal of a Naturalist*. 1830.

Lipson, E., *The History of the Woollen and Worsted Industries*. Black, 1921.

Marshall, Norah, *Blockley Silk Mills*.

Marshall, William, *Rural Economy of Gloucestershire*. 2 vols, 1789.

Mills, R. B., *The Strongs and the Kempsters*. Private Ms.

Playne, A. T., *History of Minchinhampton and Avening*. 1911.

Riddelsdell, H. J., Hedley, G. W., and Price, W. R., (eds), *Flora of Gloucestershire*. Cheltenham, 1948.

Rudge, Thomas, *General View of Agriculture in the County of Gloucestershire*. 1807.

Rushen, P. C., *Chipping Campden*, 1911.

Seebohm, F., *The English Village Community*. 1890.

Shorter, A. H., *Paper Mills and Paper Making in England*. 1957.

Verey, David, *Gloucestershire: The Cotswolds* ('The Buildings of England Series'). Penguin Books, 1970.

*Victoria County History of Gloucestershire*. Vols 1–3.

White, J. W., *Flora of Bristol*. 1912.

## GENERAL

Brill, E., *Old Cotswold*. David & Charles, 1968.

Brill, E., *Portrait of Cotswold*. Hale, 3rd edn. 1970.

Evans, H. A., *Highways and Byways in Oxford and the Cotswolds*. Macmillan, 1905.

Gibbs, J. A., *A Cotswold Village*, 1895. Re-issued as *Cotswold Countryman*, MacGibbon & Kee, 1967.

Gretton, M. S., *Burford*. 1914.

Hadfield, C. & A., *Cotswolds*. Batsford, 1966.

Massingham, H. J., *Cotswold Country. A survey of limestone England*. Batsford, 1937.

Timperley, H. W., *A Cotswold Book*. Cape, 1931.

Warren, C. H., *A Cotswold Year*. Bles, 1936.

Waters, B., *Thirteen Rivers to the Thames*. Dent, 1964.

## INDUSTRY

Daniels, J. S., *The Woodchester Glass House*. Bellows, 1950.

Derrick, F., *Cotswold Stone*. Chapman & Hall, 1948.

Tann, J., *Gloucestershire Woollen Mills*. David & Charles, 1967.

## LOCAL HISTORY

Adlard, E., *Winchcombe Cavalcade*. E. J. Burrow, 1939.

Baddeley, W. St C., *A Cotteswold Manor: the History of Painswick*. 1907.

Barnard, E. A. B., *Stanton and Snowshill*. 1927.

Carver, A., *Story of Duntisbourne Abbots*. A. Carver, 1966.

Carver, A., *Story of Duntisbourne Rous*.

Clifford, E. M., *Bagendon; Excavations 1954–56*. Heffer, 1961.

Dent, E., *Annals of Winchcombe and Sudeley*. Murray, 1877.

Finberg, H. P. R., *Roman and Saxon Withington*. Leicester University College, 1955.

Hyett, Sir F. A., *Glimpses of the history of Painswick*. J. Bellows, 1928.

Lindley, E. S., *Wotton under Edge*. Museum Press, 1962.

Rudd, M. A., *Historical records of Bisley*. 1937.

Whitfield, C., *History of Chipping Campden*.

# Index